LIVING

A

COUNTERSIGN

From
Iona
to
Basic
Christian
Communities

by
IAN M. FRASER

Illustrations by Ray Price

First published 1990

Other Titles by Ian Fraser include:

My Faith and My Job
Faith Comes Alive
Bible, Congregation and Community
Sex As Gift
The Fire Runs
Let's Get Moving
Live With Style
People Journeying
Wind And Fire
Reinventing Theology

And Hymns in many Hymn Books

The Wild Goose is a Celtic symbol of the Holy Spirit.
It serves as the logo of Iona Community Publications.

WILD GOOSE PUBLICATIONS
The Publishing Division of The Iona Community

Pearce Institute, 840 Govan Road, GLASGOW G51 3UT
Tel.(041) 445 4561   —   Fax.(041) 445 4295

Made and Printed in Great Britain by
Billing & Sons Ltd, Worcester

To Nan and Alex, Margaret and Eric
in gratitude, with love

Natalie led us across the high span of the Dom Luis I bridge over the Douro to the main part of the city of Oporto. The crags we faced were topped by the magnificent Archbishop's palace which, though now used as offices, speaks still of the lordly power which the church once exercised, and reminds us of the extent to which that ecclesiastical power is still in evidence. We reached the other end of the bridge and she gestured downwards. At the foot of the palace lay the dwellings of the poor, with cramped quarters, broken roofs.

"Every day" said Natalie "there is set out before the eyes of the people of this city this visible sign of what the church stands for. What wonder then, that we have been called to contradict that sign and to live a countersign."

The countersign is the style of life of basic christian communities in Oporto. They are small in number. They look frail. They are pregnant with the future.

from *Wind And Fire*

We gratefully acknowledge the contribution of the Drummond Trust, 3 Pitt Terrace, Stirling towards the publication costs of this book.

Basic christian communities need to be understood in terms of their historical roots, their distinctive features and their experiences of struggle. Ian Fraser starts by tracing that part of the rooting system which derives from the founding of the Iona Community in Scotland in the 1930s; then draws upon their own words to describe essential characteristics of their life; and goes on to offer some examples of their struggles and pointers to their significance. In an appendix he examines traditional marks of the church to demonstrate that theirs is a renewed orthodox faith, with a life-giving quality which is full of the promise of renewal for traditionalist churches.

They are frail and vulnerable, no strangers to failure. They are not success stories. They are gospel stories.

CONTENTS

4

SECTION 1
SIGNS OF ROOTING

TAKE-OFF POINT

If this were an autobiography, an appropriate title might be *Short Commons Next Time*. In this book account must be given of some parts of my life. The context is one of rare privilege. Such privilege has a biblical warning attached!

Over 44 years I had in Margaret a wife who was the joy and crown of my whole existence. She shaped my life in love. That such as she should have chosen to share life with such as myself adds a strong sense of awe to the thankfulness I experience. That thankfulness extends also to children and grandchildren who are wonderfully warm and affectionate and add joyful dimensions to life.

Then we have had enthralling jobs. True, the terms of many of these would have been unacceptable to plenty of others (so few seem to realise that it is through challenges which scare the pants off you that life gains relish and faith matures).

My first task — as far as I know as the very first of the worker/pastor, worker/priest breed (before even the French worker-priests began) — was a lonely and frightening venture in 1942−44. Yet there was personal sustaining. Margaret married me in 1943 when I was a labourer on a labourer's wage; and, as well as being an emissary of the Home Board of the Church of Scotland, I had backing as a member of the Iona Community.

The Scottish secretaryship of the S.C.M. which followed required the welding together into one community of people straight from school with those coming back with wartime experience — no simple task.

Thereafter we were called to serve in Rosyth Parish Church at a time when it was in disarray. A secession faction had split away and was meeting in the Co-operative Hall. Two short leets of candidates had turned the job down. We accepted the call.

Twelve years later we knew it was time to leave. Margaret was having a severe cancer burned out of her by radiotherapy in the Western General Hospital in Edinburgh when we were sounded out about moving to Dunblane to get Scottish Churches House into being — **before** money had been secured either for restoring the buildings or for our own support. Margaret's response, when she did not even know whether she would be alive at the end of the year, was 'That's for us!'

And so on. We were privileged to be placed in situations which stretched us to the limit. Faced with difficult tasks,

Margaret would take the measure of the situation, roll up her sleeves and tackle them with grace, imagination and verve. The challenges which faced us and the marriage we delighted in seemed to be made for each other.

Thus I have had a rich time here on earth. If the parable of Dives and Lazarus is a guide to what we may look forward to in the next life, then what was said to Dives applies equally to me. I have already had 'my fill of good things'. What can I look forward to but short commons next time!

In relation to what follows, note that a biblical warning is also attached to present estimates of what or who is important. When things are weighed in the balances at the end of the day, the one sure thing is that we are all in for a shock. The Last Judgement is a turn-up for the books.

A single parent who brings up a child not specially well but reasonably so may do more to shape human history creatively than I (or Mrs. Thatcher) will ever hope to aspire to. Someone who has learned to relate sensitively to a mountain or a river, the dosser who shares a crust, the designer of a Ginger Rogers dress which swirls ecstatically in the dance, adults who have learned to take the pace of a child, people who manage to survive for one day at a time amid poverty and oppression, those who give shoulders to weep on and dancing feet to share joy, tarts and tramps, publicans and prostitutes who press into the kingdom before the righteous (Matt. 21: 31,32) — all may well put in the shade anything I have been involved in. What I can do is set out some things which I had not been able to discern previously as coming together to make a pattern, which seem to me to be twined into Kingdom history. I cannot estimate, in final perspective, their importance. All I can say is that they came in on the way of obedience !

What follows is autobiographical only to the extent needed to provide particular background to a contemporary development — the emergence of basic christian communities on the world scene. I was fortunate to be present and involved in situations where some historical developments took shape and gained substance. The emergence of basic christian communities is a case in point. Scotland provided one starting point.

Over the years I had no awareness of the common thread linking seemingly diverse events I have set out. Then in March 1989 I spent three weeks in contact with Spanish basic christian communities in Andalusia. I did what they asked of me, i.e. listened to their own experience and shared information with them about basic christian communities in more distant parts of Europe — in order to provide links, offer encouragement and stimulate relationships. But then they proceeded to ask very direct personal questions. At times a Scotsman solo at times a Scottish couple had acted 'like apostles in the early church' (as the Barcelona communities had put it in the early 1970s) —

carrying news from community to community; interviewing members so that communities elsewhere might hear about the priorities and lifestyles of one another; encouraging links within countries and between countries. Where did the Scottish Connection come in?

It was then that I realised that Iona, Geneva, Rome were links in a chain of new life.

I told them about the Iona Community founded in 1938 and my membership of it since 1942;

of the development of the Department on Laity of the World Council of Churches and my appointment to the Committee on Laity at the New Delhi Assembly, 1961;

of the flowing together of Roman Catholic and World Council of Churches insights between Vatican II, 1964, and the Laity Congress, 1967, and the part I was asked to play;

of the responsibility given me by the W. C. C. for the development of one of the major programmes initiated by the 1968 Uppsala Assembly, entitled *Participation In Change*, and contacts this produced with small communities all over the world;

of the extension of this work when I became Dean and Head of the Department of Mission in Selly Oak Colleges — since basic christian communities were, in my judgement, major signs of a church renewed in mission;

on our retirement, of the assignment given to Margaret and myself by the British Missionary Societies and Boards — to subject ourselves to a common Third World experience through contacts with basic christian communities in the Philippines; thereafter to develop a programme of visitation of basic christian communities in Europe in every country, east and west, where some such development existed, in the hope of gaining insights relevant to the renewal of the church in Britain.

Out of all this emerged the book (now out of print) entitled *Wind and Fire — the Spirit reshapes the Church in Basic Christian Communities* into which we gathered the fruits of our experience. The Resources Centre on Basic Communities was established in Scottish Churches House, Dunblane. There over 200 self-understandings of these communities are gathered (a mini resource of 110 examples has been supplied to 28 centres in different parts of the world).

Once this background was set out for the Spanish communities, I realised that much of it must be unknown territory also to others. A few months before she died in 1987, Margaret said to me "There is so much we tell by word of mouth which will be lost if we were suddenly to depart. It is time we got more of it down on paper'. I knew the import of that royal 'we' when it came to writing!

This text concentrating as it does mainly on European

basic christian communities, may correct a misunderstanding. In the development of these communities attention has been focussed on Latin America. Such a focus is welcome. That continent has been long neglected and is now a major source of new light and of enlightened theology. But it is a quite mistaken idea that basic christian communities started there and spread elsewhere from that source. I can illustrate from my own experience.

In 1979 I made fresh visits to communities in Holland, Belgium, France, Italy and Spain; then in 1980 went across to make or strengthen links between them and those in Mexico, Guatemala, El Salvador, Nicaragua and Panama.

In two of the Central America countries visited, I was met with astonished questioning. 'We hear that there are basic christian communities in Europe — how can communities like ours exist in affluent Europe?' By the time the matter was raised, I had learned enough about their own situation to select communities on that continent whose experience resonated with their own and tell stories about their lifestyles. 'Incredible'! they said. 'These are our kin. Certainly they do not have the same context to work in as we do. Their young people are not hunted by the Death Squads. They do not have Molotov Cocktails thrown through their kitchen windows or against their back doors. But, allowing for the difference, they are in the same struggles as we are. How can this be? The broad Atlantic rolls between. We have not sparked them off, and they have not sparked us off.' They came to the conclusion that the development of basic christian communities throughout the world was by spontaneous combustion of the Holy Spirit.

What I tell is just one part of the whole story. When the Celtic Church developed its mission, it arrived at times in places where hermits had gone beforehand and established a presence. Twenty years before stirrings in Latin America, a 'presence' was established in Scotland through the founding of the Iona Community. In other countries and continents also there must have been harbingers, and we need to know about these. What follows is both a personal account of some early pointers to the development of basic christian communities on a world scale and an encouragement to others to identify the early signs of a new life in their own country or continent which presaged such a development.

THE IONA COMMUNITY –
A JOHN BAPTIST SIGN

Fr. Joe Healey of the Maryknoll Language School, Musoma, Tanzania has identified and recorded a great variety of names for small christian communities in our time. That must not obscure the fact that a particular development, 'a new way of being church', has found expression in those called base or basic christian communities, or basic ecclesial communities. These, for all their great variety, have features which are identifiable, so that they can be quite clearly distinguished from communities which are traditional, or merely ad hoc, or escapist from the demands of modern life, or not founded on christian faith. How is the Iona Community related to that strong line of development?

Not as a progenitor but as a pioneer. It stands as a John Baptist sign beforehand of what was to follow. In the 1930s it was charting a road ahead on which many others would later travel.

1.   It expressed the perceived need for experiments in forms of new community in which the realities of life can be faced, justice fought for and divisions overcome. It was an attempt to discover what a community of the Kingdom might look like as a sign of a church renewed for mission.

Dr. George MacLeod had developed a notable ministry in Govan in Glasgow in the depression of the 1930s. It was a time of severe unemployment and underemployment, of great poverty and, in spite of the spirit of the people, much despair. If any parish ministry was to be counted a success, his certainly was. Yet he was dissatisfied. With others he searched for a fresh creative starting point. There was a need to 'Do a new thing' in the face of problems of economic and industrial decline. The choice, under the Holy Spirit, seemed eccentric.

Some probationer ministers of the Church of Scotland and some craftsmen went to form a community on Iona, the tiny island off Mull in the West of Scotland. It was the site to which Columba and his Celtic monks had come in 563 A.D. to make a base for their mission – which extended to Scotland, then Northern England and finally right across the continent to Russia. It would be a romantic thing to follow in his footsteps! But what relevance had such a romantic impulse to the problems facing Scotland and the world beyond? In Columba's time, the sea had been a highway whereas, in the 1930s, Iona was on the margin of a country which was on the margin of a continent – a shining, many-coloured jewel set in azure seas whose water had a startling clarity, but off the beaten track and difficult to reach. All that one can say is that some people are led to situations and take initiatives which have significance beyond the obvious.

In these early years we in the Community often wondered whether we had made a mistake and should pack the whole thing up as an impossible dream.

The importance of the search for new community was represented in the character of Dr. MacLeod himself. He had a strong and charismatic personality and needed the discipline of a community to check and enlarge his vision. His instinct to manoeuvre and manipulate would break through at times and thwart the community's free development but, over the piece, many of his insights seemed right and were gladly accepted. Mutual submission was part and parcel of the re-establishment of the church as a community of faith which was like a body with many parts each contributing to the other and each receiving from the other that all might be built up in love.

From the very beginning, in 1938, the concern to draw work and worship into new relationship was evident. In the morning, those who had been trained to be ordained ministers led the worship; then they went out and served as labourers to the craftsmen; and, at the end of the day, led the closing worship to round off the total offering of that day. This not only made a unity of things which had been put asunder. It expressed the equal honour due to people who had different skills to contribute to life. Besides the rhythm of the day there was a rhythm of the year. In the summer all were on Iona. In the winter the probationer ministers worked in church extension parishes, two by two.

It was this arrangement for the winter which was the stumbling block when Dr. MacLeod asked if I would join the Iona Community. Because of my background, and a conviction which had developed during theological training, that question could not be answered directly. My father, a butcher, went blind when I was four. By the time I was seven I, and my brother who was older, got up very early in the morning to work alongside him before school to make a living possible. The gap between working life and the life of the church struck me forcibly. Besides there were those who lounged around street corners when respectable people were on their way to church on Sunday. Here were two distinct communities in one small town!

While I trained in New College, Edinburgh, this division of the human race remained with me as a puzzle and a challenge. Once my degree in theology was completed, I determined to cross the divide — with reluctance entering alien territory, but under great pressure of the Spirit. Dr. MacLeod faced me with the choice — was I going to go into a church extension parish and join the Iona Community, or go labouring in industry? I replied that, if I had to choose between the two, I was going labouring, but why should these be alternative options?* After prayer and further discussion, the community agreed that my conviction should be followed through and I should become a member. From then on, Dr. MacLeod did everything in his power to make it possible for me to attach myself to the Tullis Russell Paper Mill in Fife to be a labourer in different departments and at the same time to be a kind of chaplain-on-the-run.

In 1943, I was asked to assess some of my experience as a labourer-pastor in a supplement to the Christian Newsletter. It was entitled *Masks and Men*. In it, I made three points, two of which were edited out by Dr. Oldham in the final draft. I said that my action was not an abandonment of ministry, but a search for authentic ministry; it was not an abandonment of theology, but a search for relevant theology; it was not an abandonment of the academic, but its completion. Add these comments to the new way in which the Community was already relating work and worship, prayer and politics and you get a pointer to things to come.

2. During the 1940s, we realised that it was necessary to give shape to our life as a community. Over many years a discipline was hammered out. Elements of the discipline were tried, abandoned, reshaped, affirmed in the light of experience. For instance, when Lex Millar became deputy leader, he encouraged an attempt to use National Average income as a guide to what Community members should live on. A great deal was learned from this attempt. Although the economic discipline of the Community was eventually established on a different basis, the witness to the fact that we should not be privileged beyond our neighbour has remained a powerful factor in the Community's developing life. It has also produced an awareness which means that you will often find members of the Community in exacting and ill-paid jobs, and experimenting with forms of community life which put them alongside the marginalised. Since very early in its life the Community has been concerned to exercise a ministry of healing, yet that has never found its way into the discipline. The Peace Commitment was hammered out in the 1960s and became a Peace and Justice Commitment in the 1980s — up till then the idea of peace had too readily been assumed to include automatically the idea of justice.

What is astonishing is not that the discipline of the Community was early shaped and reshaped in the light of

* Dr. MacLeod was keen that I should become a member of the Iona Community, but I do not believe that he was trimming his sails in this instance. Persons and communities learn and grow as they encounter obstacles to the priorities they have set themselves. The Community itself experienced a new flowering when Dr. MacLeod, having played his formidable part, gave up the leadership. An obsession with ordained males as the spearheads of change was removed. Lay people, women and children came into their own.

11

experience, but that the basic discipline thus established has been reaffirmed by new members over the decades.

The core discipline is as follows:

Members take upon themselves to search in the bible for the Word of God every day, relating that Word to the situations they face in the world; and pray that they and others may be able to recognise and join God's action in the world, offering themselves for whatever might be required of their lives and sustaining other members of the Community in prayer.

They affirm their commitment to attend meetings regularly so that they keep aware of how other members of the Community are faring and take their share in shaping the Community's priorities and policies.

They search for justice and peace in the world, these being recognised as integral to the life and witness of the Community, and necessarily leading to concrete action.

The economic discipline exists as a recognition of the fact that all that we have is the gift of God and we have to use it as stewards, making modest claims upon resources in a world in which so many are deprived.

Finally, there is an undertaking to plan each day so that it is used sensitively and obediently, with a balance of work and relaxation, attention being paid to public and family commitments and to health.

So much which marks the life-styles of basic christian communities in the 1960s, '70s and '80s resonates with the life-style of the Iona Community shaped out from the 1940s on!

3.   The Iona Community has been ecumenical in every sense of the word. It is a sign that the church does not exist for itself but for the purpose God has in mind for the whole inhabited earth, the 'oikoumene'. It has also been a means of drawing churches together. Members are drawn from across the ecclesiastical spectrum. It rejects the idea that to get churches to amalgamate is enough — there must be common commitment to the things of the Kingdom.

Long before the Iona Community came into being, in 1899, the Abbey Church was given to the Church of Scotland by the Duke of Argyll on the basis that it would be restored and made available for worship by all kinds of christian denominations. (It was the outbuildings around the Abbey which the Iona Community restored). At significant points in the development of the Community's life there had been great ecumenical occasions when representatives of divided churches led worship and partook at one sacramental table providing a sign and promise of the great United Church still to come. All this was in order that the whole world might have life.

This ecumenism anticipates the ecumenism of basic christian communities. If these are found in an area which is overwhelmingly of one denomination, they are not fenced in by that fact. They will appreciate their rooting in a particular tradition and value that. At the same time, they will grow out of its denominational limitations to be an expression of the church universal.

In a statement made in 1973, the Italian basic communities at their national gathering made it clear that any kind of coming together of the churches was not good enough. There had to be at the same time a recovery of the nature of the church and a fresh commitment to God's loving purpose for the world – the church's only 'raison d'être'. Specifically, they committed themselves to the **reappropriation** of a) ministry, b) bible and theology, c) sacraments. Wherever these were alienated from the People of God, they had to be recovered, and become marks of the Church of the future.   a) Ministry is the people's work; b) the bible is the people's resource and theology the people's task; c) the sacraments are God's action with the people.

4.   As the Community increased in membership over the 1940s and 1950s, the plenary gatherings proved inadequate to give expression to the burgeoning life in Scotland and in other parts of the world. Thanks largely to the inspiration of Dr. Ralph Morton there was in the 1950s a development of Family Groups. Members within reasonably easy geographical reach of one another, along with spouses (who were often not members) met once per month during the main part of the year. Numbers worked out at about 8 to 12. The main purpose was to keep one another up to scratch about the observance of the discipline and to support one another, sharing the joys and sorrows which came to each in the way of obedience.

A meeting would begin with the Community's form of worship. There would then be a time when news was shared. The main theme for the meeting followed, possibly some policy matter remitted to family groups from the Community as a whole, possibly a careful examination of the observance of one part of the discipline, possibly some challenge facing the national community.There would then be a time to eat together and to move from that into a eucharist with which the gathering ended.

As basic christian communities were to do later, the Iona Community realised the need for people to meet in small companies to give depth to the sharing of life and to get a wider perspective and vision.

5.   The rhythm of gathering and scattering was also common to both the Iona Community and basic christian communities. People gathered round the bible to discern an obedience in the world which they then scattered to fulfil. Everything was then drawn back into worship, praise and self-examination – in order that that might lead to more faithful witness in the world: the liturgy of adoration and the liturgy of living in the world complementing one another.

13

VATICAN II

The growth of basic christian communities cannot be understood in separation from Vatican II, a remarkable springtime which freed up not only members of the Roman Catholic but those of other churches. The Council was both a stimulation to new enterprise on the part of the churches and a threat to traditional power structures. I was conferring at the heart of the Vatican in the early 1970s when I heard an off-the-cuff conversation during a break. The gist of it was that John XXIII would not be canonised but anathematised forever if some of those directing the church's affairs had their way. The talk ended with a shrug of the shoulders: 'He opened so many doors and windows — we cannot close them all'. That verdict is being put to the test today with the attempts at restoration and the increased centralising of power and decision-making in the Vatican.

In my own judgement, the pull-back started in the late 1960s. Examine the pattern of voting of the Italian bishops during Vatican II. Pretty consistently they opposed progressive measures — and were outvoted. They saw their chance in the riots and near revolutions of 1968. Alarm bells were sounded. It was argued that the threat of chaos made it imperative that good order be re-established in the church. By 1969/70 there were signs of a drawing back from the openness and adventurousness of the preceding years. In 1969/70 equally one can discern a pulse of the Spirit in Europe leading to a spontaneous surge of development of basic christian communities in many countries — through people who had been liberated by Vatican II and sought to follow through its implications in daily life. At that very time the World Council of Churches asked me to be responsible for a programme called *Participation in Change*. It meant searching out, especially in the Third World, situations in which christians, because of their faith, were becoming agents of change. It brought me immediately into contact with the basic christian communities, which were at the heart of such creative change.

The above might suggest that the growth of basic christian communities was a Roman Catholic phenomenon. It has been substantially so, though by no means restricted to Roman Catholics. When a company of eleven people from Britain spent 16 days in 1983 establishing contact with basic christian communities in Italy, from Turin in the north to Naples in the south, some of us were taken by surprise to be told that, up till Vatican II, Roman Catholics were forbidden to read the bible personally or in groups — the text had to be mediated safely through the mind and voice of a priest. Earlier in Latin America, people had told me that from boyhood or girlhood they had been brought up to believe that, if they read the bible directly, they would go off their heads, become mad. Once people had the bible in their own hands, in their own tongue, in a modern translation they did go mad — but in the healthiest of possible ways! The bible has been a motor of change.

Vatican II produced a release of new life in the Roman Catholic church which, through spontaneous combustion of the Spirit, encouraged the flowering of the basic christian community development in many parts of the world. But that is not the whole story. Dr. Hans Ruedi Weber, who made such a notable contribution to the Department on Laity in the 1950s and '60s, confided to me his concern that the foundational work done in the World Council of Churches then seemed to have disappeared from sight. I had worked closely with the Department especially since 1961 when I was appointed a member of the Committee on Laity at the New Delhi Assembly of the W.C.C. In my judgement, the early issues of the magazine *Laity* and the Departmental work which accompanied it mark a watershed in the recovery of the understanding of the ministry of the whole gifted membership of the church. Was Hans Ruedi's worry justified? Did the work disappear out of sight; or might it have disappeared into some of the turbines of the church which generated power for the future?

In 1964, during Vatican II, the World Council of Churches was asked to appoint 15 representatives Orthodox, Lutheran and Reformed to meet with 15 Roman Catholics in Glion, Switzerland for informal consultation. The theme was 'The Church in the Modern World'. This was before the first draft on the subject was presented to Vatican II, and we had to be discreet (it could have looked to Roman Catholics like a betrayal — the renewal of Roman Catholic doctrine being subjected to outside influence). Too much must not be read into the Glion gathering and those which followed — which I co-chaired, with Martin Work an American layman, up to the Laity Congress in Rome in 1967. We had no hand in official drafts. We were given opportunity simply for an informal clarifying of minds on the character of the church and especially on the understanding of the role of the laity. But I am quite clear about this. The work of the Department on Laity of the W.C.C. and the concept of the church as the People of God met and nourished one another at that time. During and following Vatican II Roman Catholic and World Council streams flowed together.

These gatherings over four years were illuminating in other ways. The first encounter included sacramental services each day. There was a Roman Catholic mass, an Orthodox eucharist — and I was asked to conduct a Church of Scotland communion service for the third. At the end several priests were waiting at the door. 'Did you make that up? Where did the liturgy come from? How has it so many elements in it that we want to recover?' I told them that up till 1560 there had just been the church catholic in Scotland and it was on the liturgy of that undivided church that the present one drew; I told them that in the first Declaratory Article which was definitive for our understanding of our churchmanship, the Church of Scotland was both catholic and reformed. I observed that there had not been a Roman Catholic Church in Scotland until after 1560! They had never quite had it put to them that way!

I was also asked to preside at the only communion service during the Laity Congress of 1967. All other sacramental services were Masses. The service I was asked to take was an extra one, requested by Roman Catholics. What stays freshly in my mind is the different reactions of Anglicans and of Roman Catholics. The Anglicans present protested at my thoughtlessness in asking them to handle the bread and wine to pass them to neighbours — aware as I was that they could not partake; while the Roman Catholics said how thoughtful it was of me to let them feel part of the whole Action by handling the elements and passing them on to neighbours — aware as I was that they could not partake themselves.

A great gain of these four years was the friendships which accompanied the opening up of new perspectives for all who participated. For all the differences which remained, a common vision of the church in the world began to be shared. Iona, Geneva and Rome were links in a chain of fresh insight.

Basic christian communities understand themselves to be part of the People of God, God's laos. They reject marginalising designations such as 'para-churches' or 'parallel churches'. They recover the New Testament understanding of church not as a power structure but as an organic whole whose different parts build one another up in love. They affirm the biblical images of the church as body with different organs and limbs whose life is to be expended in the world; as household whose members, as different as chalk and cheese, add relish by their diversity; as building with lively stones adding to one another's strength; as Vine and branches; as God's field in which different crops can grow; as Bride prepared for the Bridegroom . . . . and so on. They reaffirm, against the Church of Power with its top-down structures, Jesus' words when he spoke of the Kings of the Gentiles' way of exercising authority 'That is not for you'. As the People of God they also reject Esau's way — they set out to reappropriate their birthright in ministry, bible/theology and sacraments. They do this humbly but determinedly, without claiming to be the only true form of the church, while insisting that they are an authentic form, cells in the one body.

W.C.C. – GENEVA –
"PARTICIPATION IN CHANGE"

In 1969 one of the links in the Iona-Geneva-Rome chain was given greater substance and firmness. The appointment to work with Ralph Young in the field of Laity and Studies for the World Council of Churches took Margaret and me to Geneva. The task was immense – namely encouraging members outwith the Roman Catholic world to appropriate their ministry, to exercise it in daily life, and develop studies which strengthened and matured them in that ministry. To it was added the concern for Leisure-Tourism which the W.C.C. had taken up. A third major task was yet added within a short time.

The director of the unit, who was responsible for the programme "Participation in Change", had to resign through illness. I was asked to co-ordinate the work. Reservations I had about doing so concerned the way in which many major W.C.C. study assignments were then tackled. For one thing they were done by intellectuals for intellectuals, and it was high time that the perceptions of ordinary christians seeking to live their faith in exposed situations were valued and drawn into W.C.C. work. For another, when a first run at a study was undertaken, it was those most readily available who were called upon – overwhelmingly from Western Europe and the U.S.A., and male. What was produced was then sent out to the ends of the earth and the reactions gathered were shaped together and made the basis of a 'world study'. I pointed out the length of time this material would take even to reach parts of the Pacific, never mind to be reflected on and produce a mature response. But, more importantly, I argued that it should be recognised that a culturally limited stamp had already been put on such studies. World studies, to deserve the name, needed to be *initiated* in different countries and cultures.

My request was that the committee of the Department on Laity look afresh at the "Participation in Change" project. Was it needed at all? If it was, how could it be developed so that it shook itself clear of the domination of studies, at that point, by North Atlantic priorities and mentalities? The committee appreciated the need for a rethink. Yes, they concluded, the study is necessary – but change it round completely. Go to Third World countries. Search out small communities engaged in creative change, in which christians are involved. Find from the christians what it has been in their faith which made them become agents of change. Bring back perceptions for the instruction of the West.

It meant contacting communities and groups where Roman Catholics and Protestants or Orthodox were working together;

17

where christians and marxists were developing some common enterprise; where christians and buddhists were associated in fresh understanding and collaboration; and so on. The point was to get alongside, listen, learn, glean insights into the christian faith from those who lived it 'at the roots'.

I experienced the combination of conviction and terror that I had known upon entering industry. I accepted that the study had now been set up on right lines. I could tackle it heart and soul. But I was again facing alien territory. How does one even begin to identify and make contact with the small groups and communities who are participating creatively in change, in unknown countries? It was soon confirmed to me that they are often not within the ken of status churches in their own land — characteristically they work on the margins of church and world. They were rarely known to W.C.C. colleagues. It was a whole new task. But how to tackle it? Previous experience had given me just one clue: get your feet moving in the direction of the threat.

But feet need to move somewhere. I adopted two measures to get started. Colleagues who had freshly visited some Third World countries to which I might go, and people from these countries who called in at the Ecumenical Centre were interviewed. Occasionally there emerged some direct lead. More often I was like an astronomer concentrating on a disturbance in the sky indicating the presence of a heavenly body on which astronomers had not yet been able to focus. Where, in this country or that, was there a ferment in which christians might prove to be constructively involved? I could go to the place of ferment and find what I might be led to discover! The second measure was a fall-back one. It consisted of identifying one or, if possible, two people who knew the country in question and what was stirring in it. It did not matter whether they were christian. What mattered was that they had quivering antennae.

On one occasion I arrived in the Ivory Coast and immediately checked with my host on the lines of investigation suggested by Geneva conversations. It became clear that they were useless — outdated or stereotype fields of inquiry. I phoned the two fall-back contacts, found them both in, talked with them — and was informed of two 'centres of animation' and given useful addresses. Within a few hours of landing, I was making for Bouaké in a big taxi-type car designed to hold 8 people into which 16 were crammed. I was the only white man travelling that way. I was given, on the way, one of the most appreciated silent compliments ever received. The woman against whom I was squashed had a child on her knee who must have been at least three years old. He was fractious. She suckled him till he became drowsy. Then, with a trusting glance into my eyes, she took off her headdress, made a nest of it on my lap for the head of the boy, and stretched him between us to sleep.

At times I undertook a journey with even less to go on than was the case in the Ivory Coast. The whole enterprise had to have a strong prayer commitment as a constituent element. This was never clearer than when I was venturing into quite unknown territory.

In Venezuela I had been told of a community being established among the slum-dwellers in the hills around Caracas which was thought to have a significant christian dimension. This I learned at Barquisimeto, where my base had been the centre of a Pentecostal community. I did my best, there, to get some link into the Caracas situation but without success. Waiting at the airport, and as I walked to the plane, I berated God: "I've done all I can to find what line to follow once I get to Caracas and have come up with nothing. A covenant's a covenant. Get off your tod and do your part". (Were some of the biblical stand-ups with God rougher than the reporters suggest?).

The plane was only half full. The pilot was a show-off and took it up at a steep angle. I had laid a plastic file on the empty seat beside me. Unbeknown to me it slid through the back of the seat and went down several rows, landing at the feet of a young lady. When the plane straightened out she came forward: "I think this is yours". I thanked her, saying I had not even been aware of the loss of it. She went on "It has given me the excuse I wanted to speak to you. I think I have seen you in Geneva, in the World Council of Churches building". I invited her to take the empty seat beside me, meanwhile racking my brains to think on which committee or commission we might have worked together — there were so many. "No, it was not that", she said. "It was just that, some months ago, I was in a party which did the hour's tour of the Ecumenical Centre. I think I saw you during that visit." So we talked. I found her home was in Caracas and asked what she had been doing in Europe. She was just returning from a year's course in Social Work. What was her own job? She worked for the City Council. But what kind of work did she do? Quite a variety, but one of the main elements was liaison between the Council and slum-dwellers in the hills around.

Whenever possible, I sent a letter ahead of visits, making two points. I had no intention of staying in a hotel, and would be grateful for a space to sleep at night — the bare floor of a shack or shanty would do fine if there was a corner in which I could curl up. Also — I would be grateful for a small share of their own food. I was fortunate. Starting this venture when I was already over 50 I found I had a body adaptable to these rough conditions. Teak was the most unyielding base — cement is often hand-laid in the Third World and is not so rigid. I carried with me a small medical kit. When I took off my shirt in Sri Lanka on one occasion, after a night in an Indian down-town area, those present gasped at the mess of mosquito and bug

19

bites on my body. But every night I disinfected with T.C.P. and, once given a chance, the sores healed quickly. Stomach upsets were rare and easily dealt with. The gain of this way of relating to people in slums and shanties and various kinds of villages and settlements was out of all proportion. In no time trust developed which meant that people shared with me, or with Margaret and me in the Philippines, their struggles and hopes and fears and what their faith meant to them. That would happen over a day or two whereas, had I/we stayed in a hotel and visited daily, it would not have happened at all in weeks.

Here I record my conviction that W.C.C. executives, who take a plane at Geneva, arrive at another airport, take a taxi to a hotel or conference centre such as you may find in any part of the world, and return the same way, rob themselves of something which should be an essential element of W.C.C. work — close contact with the people. One of my first moves on landing in a strange country was to examine the transport systems which the people of the country used so that I could rub shoulders with them as I went from place to place and get a feel for their life. Too often what is aped is the status way in which international executives in secular fields go about their work.

So it was that, from 1970 on, Geneva fulfilled a particular role in assessing the significance of communities developing at the grass-roots, in which christians were becoming creative agents of change. Basic christian communities featured greatly, providing marks of a church renewed from below. The early enterprise from Iona, the Geneva initiative on laity, Rome's recognition of the ministry of the whole People of God in Vatican II, were given a certain modest substance and dimension by the "Participation in Change" programme which showed how, all over the world, ordinary christians were living the faith with fresh purpose in new communities of venturing.

SELLY OAK AND DUNBLANE

In 1973 I was invited to become Dean and Head of the Department of Mission in Selly Oak Colleges, Birmingham. Philip Potter, then General Secretary of the World Council of Churches, urged me to accept the appointment, but equally urged me to complete the "Participation in Change" programme. So for the next two and a half years I worked in double harness. The fruits of the programme were presented to the Nairobi Assembly of the World Council of Churches in 1975. I felt then that I had fulfilled my remit. It seemed to be time to turn my attention away from basic christian communities to other pressing matters.

But, once we got down to consolidating the existing framework of a Department which had been formed out of separate colleges, my colleagues and I at Selly Oak had to rethink priorities for mission and mission training. To work at this at the level of theory was not enough. We had also to ask where, concretely in the world, mission was coming alive. That brought me straight back to basic christian communities. What signs of a church renewed for mission were more compelling? So it came about that, this time as Dean of Mission, I renewed and extended contacts with basic christian communities in different parts of the world. This continued until retirement in 1982.

But that was still not the end of it. On our return to Scotland, I was invited to work voluntarily with the Scottish Churches Council as research consultant. It was made clear that it would be part of the mandate that insights from basic christian communities should continue to be sought and contributed to the churches. A responsibility for ensuring good contact and communication between the Scottish Churches Council and the Iona Community was also written into the job description. Concurrently Margaret and I were asked to do a particular job for the British Missionary Societies and Boards through their instrument the Conference For World Mission of the British Council of Churches. We were asked to spend six weeks in the Philippines, in touch with basic christian communities, to get a common third world perspective (I had been there three or four times previously). Then — for three years in the first instance and a further two years if everything worked out — we were to visit basic christian communities in every country in Europe, east and west, where they were known to exist, to glean insights which might be pertinent for the renewal of the church in Britain.

The requirement that we concentrate on Europe was perceptive. Countries on that continent are relatively similar in character and complexity. An immediacy of impact made the situation different in the Philippines. Small groups of poor

21

people with access to the bible in their own tongue saw **themselves** in its pages especially in Jesus' parables. They were the ones who would go out fishing all night and catch nothing. They knew the desperate loss of a coin and the joy of its recovery. They appreciated the importance of light, and salt and leaven. Stories of landlords and questions of tenants' rights which filled Jesus' parables were their daily meat and drink. The complexity of our lives in Europe does not allow such straight and simple identification with Jesus' characters. For Britain the development of European basic christian communities would be more directly illuminating. Moreover, at that time there was relatively little knowledge of European basic christian communities and their styles of life. To learn more about them would fill a gap.

The fruit of the work undertaken for the Conference For World Mission is set out in the book which we produced jointly *Wind and Fire — the Spirit Reshapes the Church in Basic Christian Communities* (264pp). The book is now out of print. This publication attempts to give some of the meat of it in much shorter space. The Resources Centre on Basic Communities, established in Dunblane, provides a more substantial and substantive reference study-source. In it are gathered self-understandings of communities in Africa, Asia, South and Central America, U.S.A., Europe — culled from 1970 on — nearly all of them given in interviews during personal visits which could extend to three or four days living with them in their situation. The testimony of the Gentle Bunyip community is, as we go to print, being supplemented as the result of a recent visit to give an adequate representation of the Australian development, which has looked to Dunblane for much of its resourcing.

Margaret died when the Resources Centre was almost complete, when *Wind and Fire* had begun to make its mark, when we had developed direct face-to-face means of communicating what we thought was important for the renewal of the church in Britain, and when we were within sight of completing the five-year task. Three months after her crowning I was able to round off the programme, establishing contacts with christian communities in Hungary. I was advised in Czechoslovakia that the best approach was to get into being an East European Congress which could later link up with a West European Congress, so I abandoned any attempts to involve Czech groups through approaches from the west. Events may well now have made this advice out of date. A fully European Congress may be, much earlier, a realistic possibility.

THE GORBALS GROUP, GLASGOW
Interview with John Harvey, 1990.

IMF: How and when did the Gorbals group start?

JH : It began in 1958. The plan to start the group had been put forward in 1954 but Glasgow Presbytery was pretty unhappy about that and so the three founder members decided to shelve it at that point and try again. In fact they tried again in 1957 and this time, largely with the help of Ralph Morton of the Iona Community, the Presbytery supported the idea. So it actually started in 1958.

IMF: Did it matter that presbytery should have supported it?

JH : It mattered to the members of the group at the time because their original proposals really were to set up little house churches. As they put it in one of their founding documents, they wanted to enable small local congregations to emerge, centred on the sacraments and on preaching and on worship, by, first, meetings and pastoral groups. In order to do that they wanted to have the blessing of the church to which they all belonged which was the Church of Scotland. They had surveyed the local parish churches in the area and found that most of the members came from far and wide and had very little connection with the area. So they wanted, as it were, to offer alternatives (I think that's the accurate way to put it) to the folk in the area. One of the problems they ran into right away was that the majority of the folk in the area were not Protestants — they were either Roman Catholics or Muslims and this caused quite a bit of difficulty in trying to set up these little local congregations.

IMF: Do you feel that the people in the area felt the Group was their group or a group that had intruded itself into their area?

JH : I think the answer there is 'neither'. I remember one woman speaking of Geoff Shaw and saying that the great thing about Geoff was that he cared about all the weans (children) and I think what really the people in the area saw was that this was a bunch of folk who just cared for anybody no matter what label they carried. They didn't in any way see themselves as trying to be sort of 'natives' of the area, a group identifying in a total way. Nor did they feel that the Group was imposing on the area because the Group didn't impose. That's one of the important things about the Group — it didn't impose, it really waited and listened and reacted to what people felt was needed. One of our principles was never to set up organisations springing out of our own fertile imaginations! We waited to see what the needs were and to respond to them.

IMF: People can't help coming from a middle class background;

but they can either, like Jesus, practise downward mobility or, like many others, practise upward mobility. Isn't it part of what people are committed to, whatever their background, that they cross bridges to be with those for whom life is harder?

JH : Oh yes. One of the interesting definitions or descriptions of the Group was given by an American Baptist Minister who was on placement with us from the Ecumenical Institute at Bossey. The phrase he used was 'we are seeking to answer man's longing for a gracious God by helping him to experience the reality of a gracious neighbour.' I think that was what we were in fact doing. We found that it was impossible to hoist the flag of worship and of institutional church life without people immediately seeing it as carrying a Protestant or a Catholic symbol on it. So, rather than do that, we sought the dioconia way — believing that our gifts such as they were (after all we had all had higher education which had been denied to most of our neighbours) should be at the service of the folk who were our neighbours.

IMF: At that time was there strong inter-relationship with the Iona Community? Was inspiration coming from the Community or did it come from elsewhere?

JH : Partly from the Community, but I think also from elsewhere. Two of the founder members of the Group were members of the Community at the time, and Ralph Morton, the Deputy Leader of the Community, was very supportive. I imagine that, at the beginning, others were as well. When I joined it I was a member of the Community. But I think the real inspiration for the work of the group came from the East Harlem Protestant Parish and from the worker-priest movement in France rather than from anything that the Community was doing. The Community, especially to Geoff Shaw, was really far too remote from the streets, as he put it. He tended to think of the Community as very much part of the institutional church — and I can say that George MacLeod was never any supporter of the Gorbals Group. He always felt that we were selling the pass by not running a proper Institutional set-up, not preaching on Sundays, not wearing clerical collars, not having a church building and a congregation. At the beginning the Group really enjoyed having the East Harlem experience of both Geoff Shaw and Walter Fyfe; but I have to say also that towards the second half of the Group's life it looked much more like the worker-priests in France than anything else.

IMF: Okay, we all quite properly take insights from the World Church quite outside our own place. But do you think that the Family Groups of the Iona Community were some similar kind of sign in a less committed way?

JH : Yes, I think that's fair. Molly and I were members of a Family Group and of the Gorbals Group at the same time. As I compare the two experiences, one of the obvious differences was

— within the Gorbals Group, we shared all our money, I mean **all** our money, and lived at a basic subsistence level according to the national subsistence level at the time, whereas in the Family Group it was more a 10% thing, you tithed your income. In the Gorbals Group obviously another thing that made a difference was that we were very local — we were there because of the area and the people in the area — whereas the Family Group was much more of a kind of support structure for folk in different though neighbouring areas and in different jobs. So there were quite substantial differences . . . . . for myself I am quite clear that I couldn't have survived living and working in the Gorbals if it hadn't been for the support of the Group there. I think the Iona Community Family Group system has the same kind of idea, to give support. Also one of the great strengths of the Gorbals Group was the rigorous accountability that we had to each other. We had to account for our weekly expenditure to the last penny and for our weekly use of time. The Family Group system as you know has a similar sort of accountability structure although not as rigorous as the Gorbals Group, whose style was much more deep-searching whereas the Family Group's is more relaxed.

IMF: How did you come together? Did people see the same need at the same time or what? What brought you together, were you friends — how did it happen?

JH : Well it happened originally because of both Geoff and Walter experiencing the work of East Harlem Protestant Parish in the early '50's in New York; and both feeling — I think independently at first and then putting their heads together — that this was a good way to evangelise within the broken-down inner city situations of Scotland. When they came back they canvassed around a number of city areas to see whether there was one in which they could try it out. I'm not sure why they settled on the Gorbals. It may have been because Lilias Graham was already there as a church worker and was already working in a similar sort of way in the Gorbals on her own, and also because Walter knew the area quite well — I think he lived near it, he lived in Govanhill. John Jardine joined them (I think he had known Walter at University) and also John's wife Beryl and of course Walter's wife Elizabeth and their children. Then the way I joined . . . . . It came about in different ways really. I was introduced to the Gorbals by my father who was a presbytery elder. He had heard about it at presbytery and had thought at the time that I might be interested. He arranged an invitation for me to go to one of the Group meetings. I was studying Divinity at the time and went along and became more involved. Molly was drawn in because she was sent on placement to the Group from the London School of Economics where she was studying social work. She was sent there to do a placement with Lilias Graham and got involved that way. So people came in from different angles. Obviously what bound us all together was this way of being the church in an inner city area. Richard Holloway, the present Bishop of Edinburgh, was appointed to a church in the area and he and his wife Jean joined the Group. There were teachers who joined us and local housewives, although very few local people became full members of the Group.

IMF: Can you say how the Group lived its life in terms of gathering and scattering? Where did it gather together in worship? What was the christian nurture point? And in what ways were the members scattered into different activities in the world?

JH : Well, the gathering night was a Thursday night, every Thursday night of the year. It was very often held in our house because we had one of the bigger rooms. It took the following form. A shared pot-luck supper; then usually communion round the kitchen table. We did the business of the evening, which was to talk about what we were doing and what needed to be decided about various activities, or individuals; and we ended with a short liturgy of prayers of concern. During the meeting we also accounted for our weekly expenditure and received our next week's money. That meeting was a must !

You had to ask off if you worked late or if you had something else on on a Thursday. You had to make a case, and you were very seldom given permission to stay away. But it was a tremendous support system.

Then for the rest of the week we just followed our own trades and professions although a number of us used to meet quite regularly for lunch throughout the week. We had different areas of responsibility. Some of us worked full-time with the Group. Others worked for other employers. Thus, at the time that I was a member, Walter Fyfe, one of the founder members of the Group, was working for a trade union as a trade union official. Geoff was a full-time agent for the Church of Scotland working with young adults, well 16, 17 year olds. John Jardine, although he left shortly after we came, was a teacher in one of the local secondary schools. There were other people doing social work jobs. In my case I was a freelance for three years with particular responsibility for some aspects of work and for running a little newspaper. A lot of us were involved in local voluntary work as well. But the nurture was provided on Thursday night every week; and, as I say, for some of us there was a daily meeting very often at lunchtime which could sometimes go on quite long.

IMF: Do you feel it was the kind of thing that basic christian communities in Bordeaux said they were, that they broke up every now and again but they broke up like seed? How long did the Gorbals Group last and when it stopped was it a seed bed for other things?

JH : Well it lasted until about 1974. We left in 1971 and the

Group was still going then. But it came to an end about 1974. I'm not sure we can say it was like seed when it broke up. It broke up partly because the Gorbals broke up. The Gorbals was demolished, and a new area of the town was built in its place which still bears the same name amongst the residents, but not on the map! In a way it did work as seed because some of the Group moved out with some of their former neighbours to the areas of Pollokshields where they were rehoused. I think a lot of the influence of the Gorbals Group was on the many, many people who came to share with us in the work in Gorbals then moved away from there to do their own thing in other parts of the country, all over the place. I think of groups that sprang up in Easterhouse in Glasgow, in Muirhouse in Edinburgh and West Pilton in Edinburgh. I think that was more the line of influence — a very wide influence, because at that time we were the only group operating in this way. Since then there have been a number of small stair communities, Columban Houses and so on that have certainly fed from our experience in various ways.

IMF: Did the traditional church learn anything from the experiment or did it just feel 'well that's something we can safely wrap up and put in the bin now'?

JH : I'm afraid that the church doesn't have a very good approach to this sort of thing. It always called us — partly because we always called ourselves this, and partly because it suited them too — 'an experiment'. But it wasn't really an experiment in the sense that an experiment is normally thought of — people setting up a particular series of circumstances in order to find out particular ways a development might happen. There wasn't any real attempt to analyse and discuss some type of way forward. There never has been on the part of the church, apart from one honourable exception. Nor was any interest whatsoever shown by any of the Divinity Colleges of the Church of Scotland, except St. Andrews. We had very little interest from any of the committees of the church with the honourable exception of Horace Walker and the Home Mission committee of the Home Board. There were one or two people in Glasgow Presbytery who were interested, but very few others as far as I could see. I think that what we were actually doing was not experimenting at all, but exploring new ways of forming the church. We didn't see that clearly enough at the time. If we had I think we would have been bolder.

It disappoints me that there's not a lot of exploring going on within the church. There maybe are one or two experiments. But there surely needs to be an awful lot more exploring with the church encouraging people to take more risks in the way they relate to the new world situation, the new society that's emerging; risks more in terms of the upward mobility and the downward mobility of people, much more exploring to see what God is doing in these areas with people. At the moment the church is still far too closed up, far too keen to have everything set out very clearly before it moves. I don't think that you ever find out new parts of a country if, before you move, you've got to have everything mapped out in detail. You have to go out with a certain amount of faith, a certain amount of risk. I think that's what we were doing although we didn't see it clearly at the time, and I don't think yet that the church has really cottoned on.

IMF: Is that how you'd explain the fact that you set out to form small congregations and didn't succeed? Was the non-success a sign that you were really like explorers not knowing what you would find or what you should find?

JH : That's how I would explain it now. I didn't at the time, because I was very confused myself. I suppose when you're right in the middle of it you don't know what's going on half the time. We set up the Group at the beginning thinking we knew more clearly where we were going. We discovered very quickly that we were not clear, once we encountered the reality of the people and the circumstances that we had to deal with. We then went on to respond to people's needs and to their leading; and in the bygoing we found out a lot of interesting things, some of which had been picked up much more by people in the other caring professions than by the church. I'm sorry about that. And I'm hoping that there still will be a possibility for the church to learn from some of the things that we found out, even from mistakes, particularly from our mistakes.

THE STANDING-GROUND OF BASIC CHRISTIAN COMMUNITIES
In Their Words

To romanticise the growth of b.c.cs. in different parts of the world is both to devalue them and to devalue our various specific callings. All of us are thrust into life at a particular time and place which are not of our choosing. The terms presented by that time and place are those in which obedience to God must be wrought out. These terms are what we must concentrate on. It is a diversion from real obedience to start with bright ideas for the shape of Christian life today suggested by developments in some distant part of the world which do not relate naturally to our own situation. For it is our own situation we are given. It is our own situation we must understand. It is there that our faith must be expressed.

Suppose that, in every other part of the world, basic christian communities were proving to be the decisive model for the reforming of the church today. That fact gives no ground for assuming that the model is appropriate for wherever we are. a) We are never excused the task of assessing the 'creation factor' — the terms the world offers for obedience at the particular time and place which we are given. We are committed by our faith to analysis, research, quivering antennae, an instructed instinct, a sensitive 'feel' for how people respond in situations, a prophetic discernment of the significance of events: all these tested, sharpened and checked in community. b) We are equally committed by our faith to the 'revelation factor' — the task of probing God's Word and will. With others we must search the scriptures, expose ourselves to God's telling initiatives through history, and to insights which speak to our own condition; listen to those with skills of scholarship, of living, of suffering which may deepen and convert our own perceptions of God's will and way. We are committed, finally, to the task of wrestling with others to discover how all this may become light on paths we may take, and dynamic power to enable us to share in God's transforming work.

Once this is done, if the b.c.c. development speaks to our condition and our need, the gain is immense. For we live in a world church whose struggles and insights may instruct us in the way of Life — once we have set foot on it, starting where we are.

A Basic Form of Church?

There are three words which seem to me to be decisive

about how the church should live in the world — all of them centred on the Greek word *oikos.*

The word plain and simple means 'house' or 'home'. The gathering of christians in the early centuries was in houses. Christianity was not an official religion and was spared the need of having its own temples. The gatherings for eucharistic worship, fellowship, reflection on the bible, discernment about how to live the faith in the world would take place in small companies in ordinary houses; and, at times and places, in larger companies where someone with wealth and status had become a christian and made space for meeting available in a more ample residence. It was through churches meeting in people's homes that the faith developed and spread in the early centuries.

The second word is *paroikia,* or parish. Its meaning is a staging point on a journey. You might think of it as an oasis where animals can be rested, water supplies replenished, sick given the chance to rest and recover, and maps consulted in preparation for the journey ahead. The parish, in this tradition, is essentially a gathering-up point and a planning point for further advance.

The third word is *oikoumene,* 'the whole inhabited earth'. All that the church does in the *oikos* and the *paroikia* is in favour of the *oikoumene.* The church does not exist for itself but for God's whole beloved creation.

You will note that I am wary of people romanticising b.c.cs. or attaching them as exotic material to their existing faith-perceptions and lifestyles without changing these fundamentally. But I become more and more convinced that these communities point us to a form of the church which is in need of restoration throughout the world. Members of the church can come to parish activities and worship and return without making really significant contact with one another; or, if they make contact, it is only occasional and superficial. The church in the house provides means for such people to go deep with one another and to go deep into the faith. Then the parish can be a place transformed, as small communities feed into it the prayer and preaching, the sufferings and hopes they have shared, the discoveries made and tested in community giving fresh perceptions about the Word and will of God: and return, nourished, to battle on. The household of humankind would be served with greater commitment and greater understanding.

A special opportunity exists in new housing areas where one can plan from scratch as in *Akkonplatz, Vienna*:

"There was a deliberate decision **first** to develop a community, on the basis of which the parish could be built up. The spark came from a priest and some people who had been with him in communities previously. The community here made plans for a parish building on the basis of its experience of **what was needed for making community**. The people who participated in this were people who had difficulty in remaining in the old structures.

". . . . . . The old community did not disappear — on the contrary it gained much more self-confidence at the time of the founding of the parish. On the other hand, of course, the parish could not be a community in the way that we understand the word 'community' . . . . It is our aim that the whole parish should consist of many little communities (already there are two, one meeting on Saturday and one on Sunday, the latter the new one).

"There is now a structure, the institution is like any other parish in the Catholic church with a parish priest and a parish council. But the parish council in this parish is formed entirely of members of the b.c.cs.; and all discussions and decisions to be taken in the parish council have first been discussed and decided in the basic communities. The parish priest, of course, is part of all these communities and structures as well, so this all works together."

(Is the hierarchy happy?) "They would tolerate it, but not understand . . . . But they are happy to see life, and they feel it when they visit. They only ask us to avoid 'far-out' liturgical experiments".

A vivid expression of the new life brought into parish worship was experienced in a Sunday service in *Iglesia la Merced in Managua, Nicaragua*:

"When it is time for the sermon, the priest developed a biblical theme for four or five minutes and then handed the microphone to members of the congregation who indicated that they had something to contribute to the building up of the sermon. So the preaching was a corporate act. When it came to prayers, the priest did not even start off. Members of the congregation shouted out prayer-concerns, and the priest used the microphone to make them into prayers of the whole congregation. Alternatively, people asked for the microphone and contributed petitions or intercessions.

"It provided a rich and orderly development of worship. The secret was that about seven basic christian communities had met during the week, studied the bible theme and prayed their prayers — the parish service was where all this was drawn in and offered up."

Features: A Rejection of the Church of Power

Jesus said about the way in which the kings of the Gentiles handled power "Not so with you". Yet the church continually falls into the trap of taking that forbidden way. Those who are in close touch with basic christian communities and are aware of this failure of the church to take Christ's word seriously see in these communities a hope that the true face of the church may be given more authentic expression. If those in power positions in the churches feel threatened by this development from the base, it is because the heterodoxy of their positions is being exposed:

M. Vigli, Rome: "There always is and there always ought to be tension between institution and prophecy in the church. When the reformed churches came into being they took institutional form. For the future of christianity in the world it is essential that Protestant and Roman Catholic churches maintain institution and maintain the current of prophecy. There must be form; and there must be free authentic interpretations of gospel demand. The basic christian communities never want to be a 'self-standing', quite autonomous, church."

Tina Halkes, Nijmegen: "We must get rid of the rigid structures now existing and the hierarchical power-pyramid, and make the church in the shape of a circle."

Balducci, Florence: "1) The church has not caught up with where we are in the world today at this stage of human history. 2) The structures of the church almost everywhere reflect the structures of secular power whatever the prevailing power might be. 3) The church really acts as if the centre of the world were in Europe, whereas today a world vision is absolutely essential."

He spoke of: "Churches which are prepared to go to meet Jesus Christ, open to death and resurrection in him — which are prepared to die as the denominations they have been and face all the dangers of such a death . . . . .

"We have to found a church of and for humanity in which there is no master and servant, no bishop, no pope. This is needed if there is to be an option for the poor."

Dr. Fuchs, Berlin Conference of European Catholics: "Just as is the case with small countries, I believe small organisations are becoming and will become more and more important. Independent-minded people from different denominations who take part in these small communities are a necessary corrective to the super-power church which has too much apparatus and too little gospel charisma."

The super-power church which has too much apparatus and too little gospel charisma.

"A cup of water? I'm terribly sorry, but it's more than my life's worth to leave what I'm doing."

32

Basel b.c.cs.: "I think that God — in Basel especially, although I hope also for the whole of Europe — wants us to go against the spirit of the times and develop new, disciplined communities."

When there is a crack-down, the result may be new life:

Vomero b.c.c., Naples: "Because people were encouraged by him to vote according to their own instructed consciences in the 1974 Divorce Referendum, Franco (the priest) was pushed out of the parish. A b.c.c formed around him. This was the real start of the b.c.c. The church was understood to be the People of God who contain within them the hierarchy. They met in one another's houses."

Padeo de Legua b.c.c., Oporto: "The official church was shut in on itself, living for itself . . . . . those who came to church just came and went, making minimal or anonymous contact with one another. For thinking young people it made no sense. Life was somewhere else.

"After the revolution there was a contrast between those looking for a new way and the traditionalists. When it came to the crunch, there was a class division, the rich siding with the bishop and the poor with the new way. The priest stayed with the latter. He was cast out. A b.c.c. formed round him and met in a garage. The celebration then was of the Word — to celebrate the eucharist would have distanced them from the parish, and that they did not want."

The basic christian communities do not seek to distance themselves from other forms of church life. They speak of themselves as expressing 'a new way of being church'. This does not exclude other ways of being church. What the b.c.cs. insist on is discovery-space to find what it is to live the faith in the world so that they might understand better what that faith is. They believe that in carving out that space, they are making a contribution to the renewal of the whole church as they would not if they were simply absorbed into the traditional fabric and activities of the churches. Then, once 'discovery-space' has been secured, classes alienated by the church in its traditional form may find a place:

Guimaraes b.c.c., nr. Oporto: "The official church is distant from real life as people have to live it daily. The b.c.c. seeks to practise Jesus' way as a way related to people's daily life . . . . We are a church of the people, of working people not alienated from what makes up their lives . . . . .

"Official communications about faith and life are made up by the hierarchy *ex cathedra*, not worked out in the church. People are needed simply to pay their dues to keep the system going. They are given no voice. They have no lively faith. The b.c.cs. in contrast are a ferment among the people."

Linz b.c.c.: "They are people who have not felt at home in the institutional church, and feel that they want to explore further

People are needed to keep the system going.

THE CHURCH MACHINE STUPENDOUSLY POLYPHONIC

COINS → HERE

"No money ! No music !"

and go deeper than the institutional church allows for."

Theo Buss, Gospel b.c.c., Neuchatel: "We do have relationships with the institutional church. Every one of the members of the clergy belonging to the group has work in the institutional church. But we try to create a space of freedom. For instance, when children were baptised into the community, we had a strong reaction from, if not clashes with, the official authorities. They didn't like it because it is contrary to their rules. But we maintain this space of freedom."

San Marco b.c.c., Rome: (Why create a b.c.c.?) "We were given no space to work out how to live our faith and think through our theology, as the parish was organised. So we looked for that space, at the same time carrying out our parish responsibilities.

". . . . . But we were pushed away! We were not allowed to remain as a parish group seeking new ways . . . . . We had to face difficult pressures in the 1970s wherever we simply insisted that adult christians should be free to make their own choices (on referenda on divorce and abortion, and an option for the Left.)

(But they still meet in the hall. There is a good relation with the bishop who acts as mediator between the b.c.c. and the parish. He is more progressive than the priests).

"We know ourselves to be church and part of the whole church, but the institution does not recognise this . . . . . We respect the institutional church structures but they do not respect us — that is the position."

Marcello Vigli: "Dialogue is opening up in the parishes and between St. Paul's and the hierarchy. . . . . . The b.c.cs. have never asked that the parishes **become** b.c.cs. What they ask is that they be given space to live their lives authentically, so that authenticity may penetrate into the church and help it to renew itself. . . . . A good part of the Latin American hierarchy is . . . . behind the b.c.cs. and that kind of conversion is needed in Italy."

Juan Garcia Nieto, Barcelona: (about rural workers with a strong folkloric faith, moving to cities) "They will keep their faith here, inside this new industrial culture, they will never think of building a church apart from the interests of the working class . . . . . There is a qualitative difference between what happened 30, 40, 50 years ago and what is happening now. Now the working class can find a type of church through grass-roots communities which links their own interests to a new reading of the gospel."

Some Brief Perceptions.

Oregina b.c.c., Genoa: "The church is . . . . . ordinary people trying to live the faith seriously and in freedom."

G. Delteil re Beziers b.c.c.: "There was a marvellous combination of work on a subject of concern, a celebration and eucharist in which all joined, and a meal which made an expression of deep fellowship. All these things belonged together. The bible is read and then worked over and commented on by the people taking part in that celebration. So the bible is always opened so that they might get light on the work they are to do."

Oporto b.c.c.: (Answering the question — What attracted you to the b.c.c.?) "a) a very profound sharing of life, of personal concerns, of goods; b) 'fraternal correction' — outspoken, honest mutual taking-to-task when believed necessary; c) solidarity with humanity — those nearest and those further afield in the world; d) the reading of the bible for today — the gospel and the Acts show 'a people for freedom' who share all things."

Manuela observed: "The main characteristic is sharing: the sharing of life, goods, food, personal troubles and hopes, homes — all springing from the sharing of faith, bible, eucharist."

G. Franzoni, St. Paul's b.c.c., Rome: (Features:) "a) attentiveness to the bible as the Word of God and to the eucharist; b) a relating of the movement to the institutional church of all denominations; c) alliance with the working class movement and organisations bent on liberation; d) relocation — to be alongside the marginalised and suffering, the under-proletariat."

Being in the World as Church
Christians join forces with others.

Ciro Castaldo, Naples: "The b.c.cs. have to be alongside all who are genuinely fighting for liberation. they need to be within the liberation movement of the masses, and be leaven."

Cite b.c.c., Paris: ". . . . . The christian life seems to us to be necessarily militant in character . . . . . we are ready to associate ourselves with actions of which other groups are the initiators."

Ex Quadraro b.c.c., Rome: "What was important was not to put a christian label on action but for all to be involved: in peace, trade unions, Third World solidarity."

Nico Roozen, Utrecht: (In the first phase there was a special concern for foreign workers and links with other relevant organisations): "It became quickly clear that what we must do as christians is to help people develop their own organisations in their own way. They must always liberate themselves. At the very least you should not get in their way, at best you should find means to be available to them.

"The establishing of links with the workers' organisations made it clear to us that they had a political colour which was uninfluenced by christian perspectives on life."

Livorno, a visiting team observed: "The b.c.cs. have a constructive relationship with those in local government, the docks, those working creatively to meet the needs of the city. We were welcomed at the local government offices by Ivo del Greco, a C.P. councillor, plus Maria Volpi, who spoke on the council's developing work. We met, at the Community centre, volunteer workers; then dockers at the docks; then shop floor workers, mainly women, in an occupied factory.

"A co-operative provided hope for drug addicts, psychologically unstable people, the unemployed. 'The b.c.c. has learned a great deal through those in the co-operative'."

Brignais b.c.c., Lyon: (What advantages are there in belonging to secular groups?): "One advantage has been that in the group it has been possible to meet the kind of people one would not come across in the parish structures of the church. Accordingly, when we are going to initiate a movement concerning peace in the world, there have been people that we were able to draw into this from a wider range of members of the broader community. The content of the work in preparation for this day of peace has been contributed by all kinds of members of that community."

Vomero b.c.c., Naples: (The group was very aware of the way in which, through the gospel, the church grew more in touch with social reality): "There are communities, especially in Southern Italy, where the poor and marginalised are members alongside those we call 'intellectuals'. This seems to happen where all together are attempting to make radical changes in the whole of society. Where the concern of a group is merely radical change in the church, the marginalised do not get involved. (A workers' co-operative started in Calabria in the face of the Mafia). B.c.cs. in the region of Naples have become a kind of point of reference in social, cultural and political issues for those who are developing a new awareness, a new conscience."

Padeao da Legua b.c.c., Portugal: "Let me put it simply: being members of a b.c.c. allows us to live in the world the claims of the gospel.

"For me it was a matter of growing in understanding of the length and breadth, the height and depth of the liberation God has prepared for us."

ORTHODOX FAITH IS RECOVERED AND LIVED

Jesus Christ is central:

Ciro Castaldo, Naples: "It is Christ who summons the communities into existence and draws the members together."

Community of the New Way, France: "We are all in unity because we have all lived through an encounter with Jesus Christ which has turned our lives upside down."

Open Letter, Cite b.c.c., Brussels: "In Hebrew only one word is used for 'community' and 'testimony' (which is in favour of the one who has raised up the community and keeps it together) . . . . . the community is, by its art of living, the living remembrance of Jesus, a witness to him by its life . . . . . in this Spirit of truth, basic communities are not sociological accidents. Jesus brings the community together. The community is the place where members take root in the Universal Church. While living and actualising this reality, they are constantly and actively aware that they must create, guard and maintain contact with all other communities of faith. If we believe that the community has been convoked by Jesus Christ . . . . . then the community is the faithful answer to Jesus' call and thus receives authority and becomes a place of mediation."

The bible has fresh place and authority:

Ciro Castaldo, b.c.cs technical secretariat, Naples: "The fundamental thing for the groups is the reappropriation of the Word of God. The bible has to be read by the People of God in light of the historical experience which is a present reality for them — which makes the bible reading a very concrete activity. The expert, the theologian, has a place **within** the community acting thus. The expert has to be the one who has shared in the community as it seeks to live the faith. In such a living context, and there alone, the historical-critical knowledge of the text provides an important contribution. Let me repeat — the place of the bible is absolutely fundamental in the life of the b.c.cs."

Turin b.c.cs.: "A different approach to the bible, to the New Testament, was needed, open to the people. It needed to be made the basis of living. It needed to be interpreted from working-class perspectives. People began to see the New Testament as a message of liberation not only for the working class but for all mankind, through struggle. (Till now the bible has been regarded) . . . as a mysterious book to be kept in the hands of priests."

Oporto b.c.cs.: "The true place of prayer is where the actual situation people have to face and wrestle with meets the bible. Q: How would you describe the community at the time of the revolution? A: I would say simply that they were 'people journeying with the bible', seeking to discover how the bible is to be situated today, for instance in relation to our present political context. The bible is a source of illumination: . . . . . when it is read without defensiveness, and is allowed to make its authentic impact. It penetrates to the marrow in its challenge to us to live life like Jesus' – really and truly like his.''

Kaufmann, Biel/Bienne b.c.c.: ". . . . . the struggle is to live life in the terms of an encounter with the bible. Here what is important is to live in solidarity with people in one's own area, in one's own region, in one's own country and in the world as a whole . . . . . Everyone is committed in a sector of society . . . . ''

Andalusia b.c.cs.: (Regarding the bible) "It is the central and permanent point of reference for all the thinking and the action of the groups. It takes a crucial place in helping Andalusian people to do battle for the future of this region. The bible is read before the celebrations we have, and then studied afterwards. 'The biblical witness is related to Andalusian self-government; and people's concrete problems – especially the exploitation of labour and the need for the redistribution of land (title to enough to support a family), unemployment due to industrialised farming, and immigration to other parts of Spain and to other countries. Many co-operate with one of the most powerful trade unions, the rural workers' trade union, and occupy land when people lack it and are suffering hunger.''

Enderestrasse b.c.c., Vienna: "The bible is the basis of our Christian life . . . . b.c.cs. in Brazil have taught me that it isn't necessary to study very much to understand the bible. It's more important to pray, to meditate the bible and to act accordingly; to involve yourself in social life and society and to fight (though not with force, not with violence) for more justice in this world. I don't think we do this enough here in Austria. That is something that we need to learn.''

Padeao da Legua b.c.c., Oporto: "To root daily life more effectively in the Word, we have divided into four according to the places where members live, so that they can address themselves to particular local situations as well as to larger issues. [The bible shows] the feeblest, the least have their part to play in God's action to liberate humanity. We find that astonishing and exciting.''

Oporto b.c.cs.: "We interpret Mary's virginity as her utter availability to God, and to no-one else, for what he wanted of her. We are not bothered one way or the other about questions of her physical virginity. Here was a life given for others. She was to bear a Son who would not be her own. She was available to God for that.

"She is being used by men in power in the institutional church to supply a pattern for the ignoring and marginalising of women. Some of us think that the gospels provide no challenge to what was the traditional valuation of women before, others that they provide radical challenge — for instance, women were the first missionaries of the New Dispensation, witnessing to Christ's resurrection."

Chris Smitzkamp, Salland b.c.c.: "Every time we go to the bible, we have to reckon with a thick layer over it of traditional and ideologically-slanted interpretations. I give one instance from our b.c.c. It concerns the widow who put her last coins into the treasury of the temple. Traditionally she is supposed to have acted well and traditionally Jesus' words are of praise for her. When we look more closely, we believe Jesus is condemning the clergy of his day for confusing a woman like this so that she gives the little money she has to robbers who demean the worship. Jesus is saying 'What a shame' "

You need to get through a thick layer of traditional interpretations...

BIBLICAL CORE

G. Franzoni, St. Paul's b.c.c., Rome: "In the St. Paul's community, five groups concentrate on bible study and use the biblical texts which the congregation will be considering at the Sunday service following. They reflect on the Word and make spontaneous (probably not very scientific) responses regarding the light it throws on life today. A sixth group does continuous bible study, and biblical scholars are members of this group. They tend to work through a book of the bible at a time. This group undertakes much more rigorous study.

"In every case the search is to discover what the Word of God is saying about the nature of the salvation we need today. They recognise that the Kingdom of God is already present, is already working through the power of the Holy Spirit."

The disinherited find new place.

Tina Halkes, Nijmegen: "We also need to recognise the limited character of 'Western, male theology' and take seriously other forms and styles of theology. Our western theology also has the limitation that it is overmuch intellectual, rationalistic and speculative in character — it rather needs to be marked by flair and spirit and wisdom. We also need to respect the experiences which come from grass-roots living. At the same time I warn against the view you sometimes find in the grass roots that theology is derived only from experiences. There are women who

39

make too much of their own experiences and relate them too little to the bible and to the rest of the human context. This is a form of *hubris* (pride)."

Passim: "What we need is ways of helping women to enter into the struggle to find the biblical message, all the while noting where women's part has been played down. (Tina Halkes' words)"

Solima sister: (contacted in Brussels, working in Pueblo Joven, Brazil) "There are very poor people there, there was no water, there was no light, it was terrible. We had to go there because the bishop did not want to renew the contract with us.One of the things which he said was 'You are not in the things which are holy' I told it to one of the women of Pueblo and she was very angry. She said 'For the bishop what is holy is all that is happening inside the church. For me what is holy is the future of my people.' . . . . .

"The Saturday before Easter I came back to my convent. It's a big convent and they had the celebration of Easter with water, light etc. There is a priest in the convent who is a very artistic man. In the Chapel there was a beautiful scene, beautiful vestments, water, a very beautiful lighted candle and beautiful music. I came from Pueblo Joven where there was no water or light. I left the Chapel and afterwards I said 'This is the degeneration of the liturgy'"

The sacraments are a fresh source of life.
The eucharist is central.

Schwechet b.c.c., Vienna: (The eucharist is) "the centre of life" "an experience without which we cannot live."

Emmaus b.c.c., nr. Turin: "There is a weekly eucharist and children, friends and guests are present. It is quite central to their life and they try to make it authentic, after the manner of the early church."

Linz b.c.c.: "The bible and the eucharist are very important. Celebrating the eucharist as we do has meant that people have rediscovered its meaning; and the fresh use of the bible has brought people alive to it as never before."

Teestubegemeinde b.c.c., Wurzburg: "The important thing is that it is the community which celebrates and not an individual pastor or group specially assigned to the task. Everyone can contribute and help in building up the worship. This allows freedom for the Spirit to take charge."

La Traboule b.c.c., Lyon: "When the priest cannot be there to celebrate the eucharist, the community celebrates the eucharist itself, because it is quite clear that the eucharist is an act of the whole community. The priest is also clear that this is so."

There is what Noel Bompois calls 'mixed practice' concerning presiding, but it is clear that it is the community which is president and celebrant, whether acting through a

40

priest or pastor, or not.

G.Koeppel, Machstrasse b.c.c., Vienna: "The priest is the connecting member by celebrating the eucharist (i.e. to the church universal)."

Akkonplatz b.c.c., Vienna: "The priest alone speaks the words of consecration — there is no pressure for an alternative at this stage of development."

Brignais b.c.c., Lyon: Q: do you normally have the eucharist when you meet? A: "If there is a priest present. At the moment, there is a difference of opinion within the community about whether a priest needs to preside. So we hold to what is possible at this stage. On one occasion, we approached the bishop and asked whether, in his judgement, the eucharist could be celebrated when there was no priest there to preside. He answered simply 'Do whatever is possible' and left it at that."

Ex Quadraro b.c.c., Rome: "A priest friend usually presides, but we also preside ourselves."

Guimaraes b.c.c., Portugal: "The co-ordinating committee listen to the total subgroup and prepare for the eucharistic celebration (getting everything in hand two weeks before it so that the plan is issued and the biblical themes can be thought through by everyone). The priest presides as the person appointed by the community, one among equals, who speaks not in the place of others but when the others give him voice."

Turin b.c.cs.: "There is a variation in practice about whether a lay person or a priest presides, but the community is clear that it is a whole people who develop the Mass as a common act — it is not a priest who controls it."

Community of the Gospel, Neuchatel: "The eucharist is an act of the whole community, including the consecration. But we ask an ordained Roman Catholic or Protestant to preside — always on our behalf and as our representative, in no way as the one who has power in his own right because he is ordained."

Chris Smitzkamp, Salland b.c.c.: "At the eucharist, the children preside with the others and hand out the elements . . . . . Anyone we trust can be asked to preside (on behalf of the whole community)."

Linz b.c.c.: "The total community presides. We, all together, say the words of consecration and the communion prayer. In the community I am not a priest over the community but a member of the community." (Markus Bucher)

Vomero b.c.c., Naples: "The eucharistic sermon is built up by the community. This possibility was facilitated by the bishop who forbade Franco, the priest, to preach. When you have the eucharist in a house that makes a difference. The way in which one person does not control it but all build it up is very important. Our life is now, as it were, 'managed from below'. In the old church we had no share. Now two married priests and

41

Franco preside together, on the understanding that the whole community is actually presiding and celebrating together."

Basque b.c.cs.: "The priest does not always preside. For instance in the regional gathering which is to take place this month, it will be the community which celebrates together, with the priest as part of the community."

Enderestrasse b.c.c., Vienna: "The sermon is not developed by the priest, but is built up by the whole congregation as they reflect on the bible and try to understand what it is saying about life. In this common sermon, any member of the congregation can contribute . . . . . Then when it comes to the consecration of the Mass, we share in part of that act. Also, before we offer up the bread and wine, there is a prayer in which anyone who cares can contribute, offering aloud his or her intercession to God."

Juan Garcia Nieto, Barcelona b.c.cs.: "If the priest is absent, the eucharist is still held every week. We do the consecration in many different ways according to circumstances. Christians in clandestine anti-Franco activity, priests included, learned to work with atheistic organisations. There was a new solidarity in the same fights. Many people said that at that time they discovered what christianity meant – to be *Hombre Solidario* . . . . . The words of Christ are always said by the whole community.

"News of struggles are read during the eucharist."

Partage et Priere b.c.c., Lyon: Q: What about the eucharist? A: "When the priest left for Bordeaux about three years ago, we had to rethink this whole thing. First question was should we get a priest parachuted in simply to take the eucharistic service? We rejected that as being unrealistic. The second option was to have one of the married priests (one of whom had been laicized and the other had not) to preside over the eucharist. That was not considered to be satisfactory. The third option was to get one of the members of the community to preside at the eucharist. This was equally rejected in favour of the decision made by the group in the end – which was to have a year when one did not celebrate the eucharist at all,

Should we get a priest parachuted in simply to take the eucharistic service?

"Now we can begin . . ."

but used the groups within the community to rethink what it meant, under different aspects.

"At the end of this period, the group decided that the eucharist should become once again a normal part of their life, and that they should celebrate it together. Those who actually handled the distribution of the elements and so on should be the two or three or four who had prepared for that evening's celebration.

"Two things in particular should be noted at this point. One is that not all members of the groups saw this eucharist in the same way, and for some it was not accepted as a genuine eucharist. The group trusted one another enough for these different views to be accepted by different members of the group. A second matter to note was that, since baptisms took place within the group, this approach to the eucharist was in conformity with their approach to baptism.

"On reflection there is a third matter worth noting. It is that, at the beginning of the summer holidays, there was no clear mind on the part of the group about what should be done. Three months later, when the holidays finished, there were differences of emphasis on the part of different members of the group and different interpretations, but the group had one mind about how it should proceed, and that it should celebrate the eucharist as a group.

"A fourth point was that instead of the eucharist being the 'hot potato' ecclesiastically, the concentration point which raised all the fears of the institutional church, it was given its place as one of the many things which belong to the life of the church, the other things such as fellowship, gathering around the Word and so on being already part of the life of the group. So this put it into proportion.

"Fifthly, the group decided to follow through its decisions for a year and then to have a rethink about what it had done. When this reflection took place, there was conviction that the way we had taken was the right one."

Baptism: the objective and the practice.

Oregino b.c.c., Genoa: "We work at unhooking sacraments such as baptism from their routine, bureaucratic administration."

Vomero b.c.c., Naples: "For baptism a different service has been worked out from the traditional one which lays so much emphasis on original sin. Now what is much more emphasized is the responsibility of the community, promises to the community, the reception of new life into the community of faith."

Emmaus b.c.c., nr. Turin: Matteo was baptised at the age of 6 months in the parish where he lived. The priest allowed them to have the kind of service they wanted, and they felt that having the baptism in that situation enabled local people to relate to the community. The community itself conducted the service.

43

Sarah was baptised at the age of 3, here, in the community not in the parish church. About 70 people attended, friends, members of the other basic christian communities etc. In this case, if they had gone to the parish church, they would have had to follow a form of service which they could not honestly affirm. Her name is not found in the parish register, but the community have documented her baptism. One result has been that the community have felt much more involved in her formation in faith. Sarah herself was a lively participant in the service and remembers what it meant to her.

Walloon b.c.c. groups, Belgium: "When a child is baptised (and they do not care for baptising babies, but children who are a year or two old) the preparation of the parents and child is for the entrance of the child into a community of several families. It is **at the appropriate point of this community's life**, and not formally into the parish or into the church that the entry takes place. A priest will be involved but he will be auxiliary to the community receiving the child. They are the actors, not the priest who is simply the assistant. A communal understanding of baptism is developing in practice."

Theology becomes the faith-basis for living, built up from the insights of a great variety of struggling and suffering people as well as by specialists.

Oregina b.c.c., Genoa: "Our theology takes shape from the faith we live. For the theology to be authentic, we have to be seen to live for the poor and not for the rich. The church must be for the last and least."

Tina Halkes, Nijmegen: "Those of us who are theological students and teachers should function among the people. The whole community should be theologians. But there will need to be some specialists, and there must always be space for those that have some new creative approaches."

Nico Roozen, Utrecht: "The subject of theology has been assumed to the bishops, councils, professors of theology etc. We discovered the christian community as the subject of theology, rather. Moreover, only communities which are playing a part in liberating struggles are in a position to make a contribution to theology. The stories in the bible are about such people."

Manuela, Oporto b.c.c.: "Vatican II has opened up the church. Theology was discovered **in the people** including the poorest and most exploited. There was not much intellectualism in the theology, just a discovery of the gospel, eyes opened to oppression, sharing of goods in consequence."

Marc Luyckx, Brussels: "Both in Belgium and in Recife (Brazil) these groups go directly to the bible, whereas we seem to need piles of books before we can start. Why do we who are rich seem to need so much writing, so much reading before we get to the biblical point which poor people reach in one step? It makes me

44

wonder what we are doing regarding understanding the faith in the west. The brazilians would say that we need to become poor and live with a big question **in our belly** to do this direct theology."

Ton Nuij, Nijmegen b.c.c.: (A member of the order was nine years in Nicaragua). "The development of the revolution and the part christians were playing in it . . . . the kind of theology that comes from the living experience of human beings at the grass-roots, a theology which did not descend from on high, all complete, from those who are supposed to prepare it for others.

Once upon a time . . .

"Coming down!"

THEOLOGY

The fortress theology of the established church

Contrasts with that of those engaged in liberating struggles

This theology at the base contrasted very much with a kind of strong impregnable fortress theology of the official church, which had no roots really in the life of its people . . . . . (it was) the discovery of a living theology among those who were struggling to make sense of life. In this theology which is coming from the basic people, the word 'liberation' is quite central."

Chris Smitzkamp, Salland b.c.c.: "We are convinced that God is present in every situation where human liberation takes shape.

The God of the scriptures both is for all people and takes sides with the voiceless people, the oppressed people whom he leads to freedom. We believe that faith comes alive not only from the revelation and the dogmatic tradition of the church but in interplay between revelation and our experiences — very ordinary, normal experiences. There are three elements — the revelation (the story, the gospel, the tradition): political engagement; and what we find from that involvement and the analysis of society. It is these, in interplay, which make up believing faith.

"Theology grows out of their interrelationship."

Partage et Priere b.c.c., Lyon: "If there were no biblical foundation, the group would not exist at all . . . . . "

Q: What place is given to theology in the group?

A: "When the priest left, and the whole business of what we should do about the eucharist had to be thought through, it was then that we started doing theology which was not handed down to us as a packaged thing, but was wrestled with as our own understanding of the faith. For one thing, the revelation of God in Christ is so totally central that everything flows from that. For another, there is no need for a developed theology, but simple bases from which life can be developed.

"The group would not be a christian group if it were simply happily working out how it would manage life as a group. It is the reference to the revelation in history which constitutes it a christian group."

Three observations from the *Machstrasse b.c.c., in Vienna*:

Trout: ". . . . the first time we had our meetings in autumn when theological questions were discussed, many people said 'Oh God, that's so theoretical, how are we to understand it?' Yet a few years later they were all wildly discussing these questions as if it was the most natural thing in the world to find out what the Holy Spirit is doing."

Andrea: "What attracted me most was Paul's type of theology — the asking of questions, the not believing in things without thinking." (Paul is the priest).

Gisela: "For some years all the members of the community had to be trained in theological and biblical interpretation. this was done, not in a systematic way but by facing questions as people raised them."

An Open Fellowship

Dutch Statement: "A b.c.c. should be a living fellowship, combating anonymity, loneliness. It should come to the help of the wandering and lost. Mutual pastoring is a collective responsibility — that covers strains in the group itself."

Villeurbanne b.c.c., Lyon: (About beginnings): "There was also freedom for people who had any problems in the way they were living their life to bring these to the whole community, and the community treated them with respect . . .

Gospel b.c.c., Neuchatel: "All kinds of people are respected here."

Christa Ziller, Neu-Isenburg b.c.c.: "A group in which I can be authentically myself."

Jesus Moreno, a Barcelona b.c.c.: "It is in small groups that you can really get deep with one another, especially in matters of faith. That size of group is quite essential (i.e. four or five, or eight or ten) — we find it possible to share our deepest feelings, the things which really disturb us."

Luogo Pio b.c.c., Livorno: Martino (ex-drug addict) : "The love and trust I have received from ordinary people has been the most beautiful thing in the world."

Kaufmann, Biel/Bienne b.c.c.: "There is the desire to share the whole of life in common . . . . . About three of four times per week people will eat with their own families and for the rest of the week they will eat with some other family nearby or have that family eating with them at their house. That's also important for the children."

Depth of relationship is not because it is people who see eye to eye with one another who have come together. In all their differences, they are trying to see eye to eye with Jesus Christ. So these differences can be honestly faced and become an enrichment. Criticisms can be humbly offered and humbly received. There is no need for class-guilt where genuine community is being established.

Noel Bompois, Paris: "The unity that you find in the basic christian communities in France is not a unity of people who have become similar in any way. It is of people who have discovered the others to be different and want them to be different and stay different so that they can contribute to the richness of the mixture when they are all together. They have their differences, but that is within the community where they can enrich each other."

G.Franzoni, St. Paul's b.c.c., Rome: "The fraternal nature of the gospel community is taken with great seriousness, and criticisms are heard and corrections made."

Teestubegemeinde b.c.c., Wurzburg: Q: In what way are house groups different from the larger meetings? What do they concentrate on?

A: "I think that the house groups should be said to have two main concerns. One is personal questions. Whoever comes to a house group can share the deepest things which can affect them personally and those with whom they are in face-to-face relationship. They know that they will be listened to and there will be a sensitive attempt to understand and help.

47

"The house groups are also responsible for preparing the service and the reflection on the Word from time to time.

"When something has gone wrong with our relationships, we propose to deal with these matters honestly and openly with one another. this does not mean judging one another, as if one were superior to the other; but accepting one another in all our guilt, anxiety and weakness, just as Jesus has accepted us. [There is a desire to be] . . . . .accepted by one another exactly as we are. We want to work at this so that we can make demands on one another and also criticise one another and still strengthen one another and stay together. (Once a year each person has to affirm adherence to this 'general position', which makes openness and truth-telling an agreed part of a trusting fellowship)."

Marc Luyckx, Brussels: "Where basic communities arise is where some social analysis and understanding of the gospel come together to provide people with a new sense of their dignity. That experience will powerfully shape any group. For the middle-class, there is no such recovery of a sense of dignity and worth to hold the group together. What binds the group is more a sense of guilt at being middle - class! (Yet)

"Here is a story for you. A young group of theologians started living in a slum in Brazil. They said 'we are really identified with the people in the slums.' But the people realised that they came from families with nice homes outside the slums; and that, every two years, the priest went back to Belgium by plane and that took more money than they had ever seen in the whole of their lives.

"The fact was that the slum dwellers were quite prepared to accept them **as middle-class** without any pretence that they were something else !

"I cannot be identified with God, or my wife, or anyone else — they are 'others'. We have to be prepared to be with others exactly as we are without pretence, and it is very important to be so. Psycho-analysis confirms this need to be true about your own identity. So it is with God — the closer you are to him, the more you know of the distance which separates you."

The Italian b.c.cs., at their meeting in 1973 and in a commission which examined the relationship of b.c.cs. to the traditional church, described their objective:

"We are working to build up a church which . . . . . is the horizontal communion of believing communities . . . . . spread throughout the world and hidden in the world as a ferment. They will be united by functional interlinking, not power, in the service of common liberation."

THE CHURCH EXPRESSES THE FULLNESS OF HUMAN COMMUNITY

The assertion that in Jesus Christ there is neither male nor female in terms of leadership and status is given concrete expression in basic christian communities:

Beziers b.c.c.: "Women and men are leading together and seeking a way out of the damaging sexist attitudes which prevail in their own church."

Basisgemeinde b.c.c., Frankfurt: "There is no privileged sex — people are asked to take responsibility simply according to their gifts."

(The Gospel community, Neuchatel uses almost exactly the same words).

G. Koeppel, Machstrasse b.c.c., Vienna: "Here the woman is quite equal to the man and there is no difference whatsoever. It doesn't matter if a woman is leader of a workshop or a man. Women's importance has grown a great deal and the women have proved that they are able to do the same work as men."

..... although this is still imperfectly realised:

Manuela, Oporto: (She was the leader at first). "I think men in Portugal drag their heels about life in community. They hold the power still and are less worried about the traditional religious positions and terms . . . . . Women question the family set-up, the power-balance in marriage etc. But both men and women in our country practice many conformities with the existing system."

Partage et priere b.c.c., Lyons: (A woman speaks). "In the community itself, we are all equal — but who still prepares the food and looks after the children?"

Nico Dekker, Dutch b.c.cs.: ". . . . . even when we men think of ourselves as well-thinking and liberal, full of goodwill, who give women all opportunities they want, the women

Women have to compete with men, yet they are always left with two tasks to fulfil.

"Why don't you take up a part-time job...?"

49

experience it a different way. I think the only way forward is for the women to do many things separately, because even the presence of men in the group prevents the women expressing themselves the way they want to. This is sometimes very difficult because it makes some men angry because they are repelled, and they feel it. But I think it is also very good for men. I have experienced this reaction in a group of men only. It is a good thing to reflect on one's attitude as men, on dominance and such things."

Tina Halkes, Nijmegen: "Women have the right to work on their own liberation since all people have a right to be full human beings. When this happens, the knife will be put into this middle-class civilisation of ours, and its many injustices will be confronted. Begin with feminism and you will be faced with a need to change all the unjust structures of the world! We must

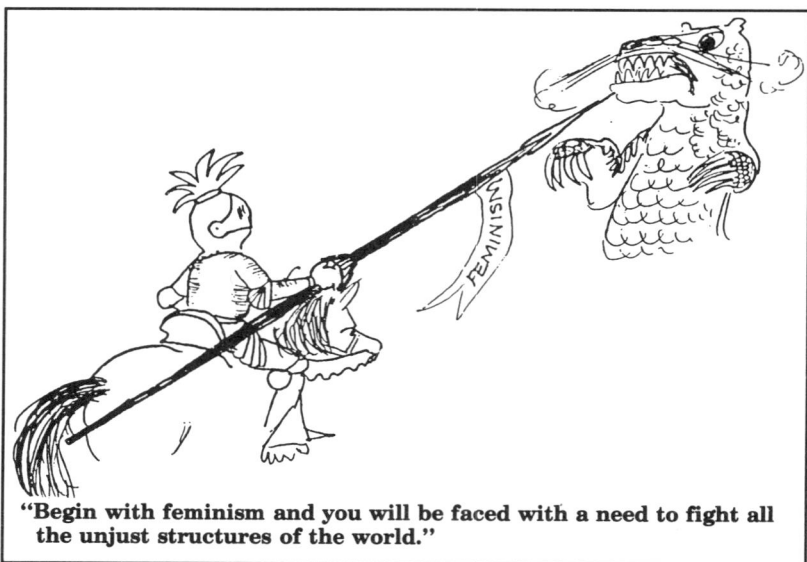

"Begin with feminism and you will be faced with a need to fight all the unjust structures of the world."

not go to the third world to tell the women there how things should be. We must empty ourselves of power in order to empower others."

Children really belong in the communities and are given a full part:

Cite b.c.c., Paris: (Statement of January 1981). "The presence of children in the community is of growing importance, both concerning numbers and quality. We take great care to associate children with us in our own searching. They take their own part in expressing things with us when they want to and can do so. In our common searching, alongside them, we observe certain guide-lines:

50

— to respect them as those who dialogue with us to the point which their capacities attain.

— to know clearly that living with them is more important than waiting to get across to them our knowledge.

"We recognise this as a difficult matter where, in spite of positive gains made over these last years, we have a feeling that we have a great deal to discover."

(In interview, 1983): "Children sometimes remain in the company on Sunday mornings. Then all together develop their biblical reflection and thinking about responsibilities of life in terms of drama or using some visual participant methods other than drama. If the discussion is likely to be 'heavy', children meet separately. There is catechesis during the week for the children."

Oregina b.c.c., Genoa: (their second concentration point: how children grow in faith). ". . . . . The adults met for one year without the children, to clarify their understanding of their responsibilities, and then met with the children again. The result is — every second week they work on high points in Jesus' life and see how these can be meaningful to children. Together they express their understandings of these high points of Jesus' life in mime, drawings, songs etc. Children have found Christ to be a living and meaningful person who attracts them and produces concrete responses in their lives. They give testimony to their faith. However, it is not the **method** used for the formation of children which have been determinative — it has been the **witness of the lives** of the parents themselves and of the whole community. The approach made with children contains within it the essence of our whole approach, which includes social criticism and criticism of our own adequacy in living the faith as a community.

"It is important for our children that they hold to values which are different from those which mark society today."

Chris Smitskamp, Salland b.c.c.: "The adults try to do everything **with** the children . . . . .(about Sunday gatherings of about 3 hours:) for part of that time the children have their own programmes, and then they take their own place in the celebration and we try to make everything we say and do such that children can understand and share in it. After the worship we also do things with the children, play with them and so on. In the service itself, they are always made free to share in prayers and make contributions to the meditation. At the eucharist the children preside with the others and hand out the elements."

Frankfurt, Dessauerhaus b.c.c.: "They have their own exegesis time . . . . . During our Word part of the service they leave us and they return after a certain time. Then we speak with them about the themes they had in their bible-thinking and we tell them about what we have done . . . . ."

Enderestrasse b.c.c., Vienna: (Family circles work with the children during the Word of God part of the Mass): "This was done in order that the children might work out, through experiences that they undergo in that time, a better and clearer understanding of the faith. It also has a spin-off in that adults get fresh insights from the children . . . . . When there are baptisms, we follow the service with a feast at which there is a great joy and which makes it clear to the parents that the child is received into a real live and large community that care for it . . . . . (Regarding first communion between ages 5 and 7): First from December to Easter, parents and children talk about the meaning of communion, so that the families have gone forward with the children, when they go forward to make their first communion."

Crista Ziller, Neu-Isenberg b.c.c.: (referring to the older child): "It came time to have preparation for first communion. The teacher was replaced by the parish priest. From what we were able to hear, the instruction was exactly the same as it had been twenty years previously, with nothing changed by Vatican II. So we were not happy about going ahead, but Catherine wanted to be at her first communion with the others, and so she went forward."

Q: And how did this work out in relation to your second child, Anne?

A: "She was entirely different. Because of that first experience, I went exploring to discover some kind of alternative teaching of the Christian faith which would be open, and allow her to find her way. There was a possibility of joining the University kind of group (the kind which would insist on three hours' discussion about whether a priest should preside at the eucharist, before developing the liturgy) but that was now a bit behind us. So we kept searching. And so we came into contact with Dessauerhaus Gemeinde which provided the community context we were searching for. At the very first gathering for worship and reflection which we experienced in this community, Anne said at the end quite spontaneously 'It is in this community that I would want to have my first communion.' "

Q: And has it remained that way with the children?

A: "Well — we have the usual distractions, interesting things on the television and the friendship of companions providing counterattractions. So sometimes they are a bit reluctant to go to the meetings of the community. But over and above all this, I feel that they feel they belong there, and they are a part of the whole community, and this matters to them. It gives them a sense that there is more to life than what simply meets the eye. They get an awareness that there are values which are different from the ones which may be currently in fashion. That is important for us."

A POLITICISED CHURCH, CONFORMED TO POWERS-THAT-BE? THE B.C.C. ALTERNATIVE.

A serious political problem is found where, as is so often the case, the church is already politicised, that is, where it brings its weight to bear to shape human affairs the way it wants. It may seek dominating positions, arguing to itself that these are adopted in God's name (when they may simply add weight to a conservative brand of politics). It may establish concordats with secular powers — which secure privileges for itself and mute the prophetic voice:

Ton Mondalaers, Brussels b.c.cs.: "The Roman Catholic church dominates 70% — 80% of the Flanders population and tries to organise christians in all aspects of life — church, political party, trade union, unions of employers, health organizations, educational organization etc.

(On returning from Chile) ". . . . To come back to Belgium was a traumatic experience, to come back to christians who were, so many of them, right-wing individualistic and liberal in the sense of being kind-hearted but without any radical analysis of the ills of society.

". . . . . Working people do not fit into what we might call 'the christian family' not because of faith, quite often, but because christians are better at organising and because christian unions are bigger and more powerful. Christians are in these because they derive advantages from being there. In this situation, it is the task for Christians for Socialism to unmask the church and show its bourgeois class basis and unmask the Christian Democratic Party and show it to be a bourgeois party. Those who come to the Christians for Socialism groups had looked upon the church as a whore, serving the advantage of the already privileged. At the same time, many had adopted the unthinking western anti-communist attitudes. Yet they have religious needs."

(Mario): "There are other communities such as Action Catholique which act a bit like the bishop's arm stretched out into this factory, that commercial enterprise. These communities are still managed by priests though those that participate may be seriously trying to relate the gospel to daily work."

Edmund Arens, Frankfurt b.c.cs.: (On Third World, refugees, handicapped): "It is difficult to have new alternative ideas in this satisfied rich and right-wing-oriented German Catholic Church . . . . !"

Nico Dekker and *Chris Smitskamp* both from *Holland* detailed different reactions of middle-class christians. Nico took note of

53

those who had a concern **in their thinking** for the Third World, but did not bestir themselves about the Third World in Holland itself.

Chris observed: "We find that solidarity with the poor and taking sides against oppression is called 'communistic, socialistic, left-wing.' We recognise our middle-class character and try to analyse our class position and bend it to the service of oppressed people . . . . .(solidarity has to be the kind **they** want which **they** define): . . . . . We cannot become one of them — we can take sides, but recognising that it is their fight, not ours . . . . . (also) . . . . .we aim to be a disturbing force among our own class."

Guimaraes b.c.c., Oporto: "In the official church, people do not stir themselves to combat injustice. They are kept passive. In the b.c.cs. people live liberation and seek justice.

"You'll find in the worship of the parish no socio-political content, no human dimension of significance. Fraternity and solidarity float in the air and move towards a sky which is without God. A b.c.c. celebrates in a way which lifts up real life — including suffering and grieving, militancy and combativeness — so that life is at one with Christ and humanity . . . . . (in) an engagement which could cost one's life."

Marc Luyckx, Braine L' Alleud b.c.c.: "With the bourgeois class, you seem to need to begin with God and end up with some concrete analysis and action. That **can** lead to solidarity with marginalised people — but it

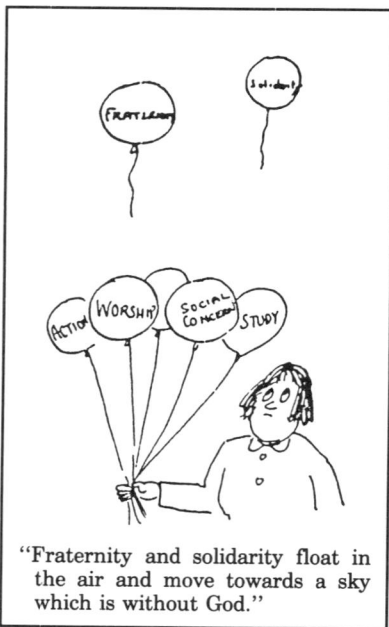

"Fraternity and solidarity float in the air and move towards a sky which is without God."

will mean that those who start that way must be prepared to lose power and money! The workers begin the other way round. They need to start with social and political analysis so that they understand the role of international capitalism and do not feel guilty as if the responsibility for present problems were on their shoulders. They are being manipulated, and they need the kind of understanding of the dynamics of society which will make them free. Then the gospel will appeal, for instance showing that Jesus' coming meant freedom for prostitutes in his time. It is at the end of all that they will discover the nature of the love of God."

B.c.c. members are encouraged to be *critical participants* in the political parties and pressure groups. They have a wide vision. Their resource is the gospel with all its challenges.They submit commitments to other b.c.c. members, open to mutual criticism and support – and then usually act these out individually or in small groups. Only rarely do communities act as a whole.

Manuela, Oporto b.c.c.: "After the revolution in 1974, there were 20 to 30 in the community. They took a fresh think about what the gospel calls for and several left a) because the b.c.c. would not be tied to one political party b) because the b.c.c. had decided to share their possessions."

Ciro Castaldo, Naples: "The communist party, for instance, has certain reservations about us. You see, we aim to be a prophetic element in every association we develop. We are not prepared to be trapped in them. Our position in political parties is such that we continue to exercise a critical voice. We find ourselves often much nearer to the masses than to the political parties, with their institutional ways."

Franzoni, San Paolo b.c.c., Rome: "We tried to get the working class movement to be aware of those who are more oppressed than they are (Third World people who can pull no weight in their home country or their new country, were specially thought about); and we want the marginalised to realise their gifts and dignity."

Ex Quararo b.c.c., Rome: "The b.c.c. 'works through issues e.g. Nicaragua, together' then each takes action 'based on common perception regarding what is needed'."

Theo Buss, Community of the Gospel, Neuchatel: "We don't belong to one political party but we have our (political) commitment, all of us, in our own set-up or context."

Nimes b.c.c.: "Members hold all kinds of political and social positions (so in the Ijmond b.c.c., Holland)."

Andalusia b.c.cs.: (About christians some years back working with an underground organisation called the Red Flag in the struggle **against** General Franco and **for** some spiritually satisfying form of life): "I think of groups in the Seville-Malaga area which wanted the church to take up a particular class stance and acted quite naively in face of political realities. It showed signs of the intolerance which often accompanies radicalism. That group was simply faded out . . . . . "

Q: Why not act politically as a body?

A: "If we took action of a concerted kind as a christian community we would be doing exactly what the institutional church does. It is a trap we do not want to fall into."

55

Basque b.c.cs.: "What we need to do is work more on the perspectives of faith which give a basis for our particular type of involvement. The group could actually lose its life, its true life, for all its involvement, if it does not take more concern for gospel perspectives."

Amrein, Biel/Bienne b.c.cs.: "Something more fundamental is needed than thinking more about the poor and sharing with them our material riches. Men and women are needed to let the good news become incarnate in themselves and to transmit this love of God by their very modest manner of living. (In Latin America) the b.c.cs. are the chosen places where poor and oppressed christians experience God's love and thus receive the power to transmit this love to others so that others also experience the fact that the love of God is a tangible reality, down to earth and concrete . . . . . Hundreds of christians have made their lives a sacrifice in fidelity to Jesus Christ and the poor."

Padeao de Legua b.c.c., Oporto: "The community has helped us to a deeper awareness of the Kingdom of God and the signs of its transforming presence in the world."

Andalusia b.c.cs.: "Peasants' b.c.cs. develop in the villages and they are strengthened by priests who work closely with trade unions. Together they present a very strong personal testimony to christian faith."

P. (a police inspector) in a Rome b.c.c.: "The questions raised by my husband in particular, and by other members of the community — from what they find in their own experience and what they read in the newspapers — are of very great importance to me. They become something like a conscience for me. When they instance actions of the police which I must see whether I can justify, I have to think twice what it is to pull on my uniform. The most significant time is when I find I have no reply I can give. Then I have to ask deep questions of myself and my job. It is my husband and my community which keep 'digging me in the ribs'. They perform an essential function."

Basque b.c.cs.: "Sometimes there are local situations which are

The intolerance which often accompanies radicalism.

so concrete that the whole community can take one line of action."

Cite, Paris: (Concerning communal action): "The community provides a springboard for . . . . . individual commitments in the world. The members have, however, acted together — in protests against the silencing of the Dominican Fr. Pohier and Hans Kung."

The b.c.cs. are committed in the world in different ways:

Chris Smitskamp, Salland b.c.c.: "We do this (analysis of our middle-class position) by sharing frankly information about our income, what we pay in taxes, how much remains in our hands — and where the money goes, what we spend it on. We can then reflect critically on our style and standard of living. It is tough, the sharing — for instance on the part of women who do not add a wage or salary to the household income to take responsibility for spending money.

"We also practice civil disobedience withdrawing a proportion of our tax to protest about its use on armaments . . . It involves writing, explaining our position to a number of officials etc. The result can be the seizure and public sale of our household goods. We can also be sent to jail — but it would be difficult for the jails to cope with the numbers now withholding tax!

"Some of us are insisting, when there is the threat of loss of job where we work, that the situation be thoroughly assessed and alternative ways of dealing with it considered. For instance, it may be possible for the rest of us to take reduced salaries so that no redundancies need to be declared."

(The group also took care for a long time of five people from Morocco, who were illegal immigrants).

Isolotto b.c.c., Florence: "The b.c.c. cares for ex-prisoners, orphans, shares in struggles for better education, housing etc. — seeking to activate the government. There has been no attempt to proselytise but to set up prophetic signs to help the whole of society to adopt Kingdom values. Members are committed in area councils, trade unions etc. They hold debates with the cultural association on matters of concern to the whole district."

Brignais b.c.c., Lyon: "There is sympathetic listening to what is on the minds of others present and, with that, a real wrestling to discover how all may relate themselves effectively to the poor. Some were prepared to live among the poor but not all were clear that that was what was commanded."

Ton Nuij, Nijmegen: (about the openness of the community's house) "We received all kinds of people who had psychological or other problems. They also gave the group a window on the world and access to what was happening in the world. As far as we could see, this showed us that the traditional way that the church operates really made no response to the basic questions bothering human beings."

Emmaus b.c.c., nr. Turin: (In Turin, before 'going rural', members were with the marginalised, prostitutes, single parents, the young). "Our relationship with the local community has been particularly good wherever we have been seen to be standing up to oppressive powers — whether they be those of the local authority, or landowners, or the church. Those who come from a democratic background are positive about us. On the other hand, those who are at the centres of power tend to look on us as a difficult and maybe rather dangerous group."

Oregina b.c.c., Genoa: (Up till 1971 they were trying to follow Vatican II and were searching): "We wanted to cease to be a community closed in on itself and to be open to the neighbourhood and to the city. All kinds of human problems and political issues, particularly concerning the marginalised, were faced, to get to an understanding of that message which gives the world meaning. We must admit that it has been easier for us to live within the community than to take our ideas and concerns into the outside world.

(They were questioned about the kind of faith response they might look for when contacts were made with people in the larger community and some service was offered): "It has been a principle of ours never to force anyone, particularly the handicapped, to become part of the community. Of course that is open to them if it is their free choice. But the fact is that, as people like that become freer and more self-confident, they feel able to move away from the community. The great thing is to get them to be full and free people. What we establish is not a relationship of giving and receiving charity! The achievement is when they gain their full human liberty.

Q: But we middle-class people need their insights and faith to liberate us.

A: "But we must not use them for that purpose. We decided not to make the b.c.c. itself an instrument for the marginalised — only too easily could we step into old ways of patronage. Working through the state, we can try to see that all marginalised people get their rights."

Another voice: "We have no right to search for our own fulfilment out of a relationship established with the handicapped."

Leiden b.c.c. Church: (on immigrants) "They are not to be assimilated. They may be the very people to enlighten the local inhabitants on who is the God of exiles. The people who think of themselves as natives are, in fact, foreign and strange to those who have come to their land."

An economic commitment is struggled with, in spite of the difficulties in finding a satisfactory form:

Padeao de Legua b.c.c., Oporto: "If you are not economically

58

committed to the poor, you are not committed."

Basle b.c.c.: Q: Do you in fact pool your income and use the money in a stewardship kind of way by providing for the needs of everyone equally and then having money for other projects?

A: "We support the enterprises of a brotherhood we are in touch with. They are monks and nuns who have projects for example in Zaire and Indonesia, and the work of that community makes on us a very deep impression and we have a good relationship to them. Then some years ago, we asked of ourselves: 'What does the poverty in the world mean to our lifestyle?' And so we decided, now some years ago, to give, every month, three thousand Swiss francs (£1,000) to that community to help support the hospitals. Now since one year ago, we try to pool all our money that we earn together. 25 people put into the pool and each of us gets the same — as pocket money, clothes money and household money. We all have the same money each month."

Trout, Machstrasse b.c.c., Vienna: "Our aim is to live in a manner which is serious about Third World poverty. If someone buys a new car, he may be challenged: 'are you sure that's right, that you spend so much money on that?' "

Partage et Priere b.c.c., Lyon: Q:Is there any communal sharing of income and goods?

A: "For one thing, it was agreed that there should be a common pool to meet the normal expenses for sustaining the group. For a second thing, it was agreed that, in the first instance, each member should put into a common pool five per cent of his or her earnings. At a later point, this was changed to a sum which was agreed by each person individually. The agreement, whether about five per cent or some other specific amount was made at the beginning of each year."

The real difficulty came with distributing the money which had been gathered. Three ways were advised within the group:

"1) Those members of the group who were in necessity could ask for a contribution to help them out.

"2) Some wanted quite individual disbursement of the funds according to particular needs which they had identified.

"3) Others believed that the common fund should be distributed to agencies which were doing significant work in the world, such as Amnesty International. So it has not been possible to get a clear policy in this matter."

RELATIONSHIP OF B.C.CS. TO THE TRADITIONAL CHURCH:

The b.c.cs. seek to recover the church as the People of God. Traditional distortions are rejected and new creative ways pursued. B.c.cs. are open to change and reformation.

Chris Smitskamp (re Salland b.c.c.): "Some were made voiceless by clergy leaders who made all the decisions. Others found the academic and dogmatic way of speaking about God and Jesus alienating . . . . . I, who had been previously a pastor accustomed to the front of the stage, found that I had to restrain myself and deliberately take a back seat — that allowed others to come forward."

G. Franzoni, St. Paul's b.c.c., Rome:
"Protestant pastors can look almost exactly like Catholic priests, in the way in which they control the church and preside at the eucharist."

Some where made voiceless by clerical leaders who made all the decisions.

G. Koeppel, Machstrasse b.c.c., Rome: "The second community has grown to maturity under its own leader, not Paul (the priest). The leader is elected every four years. If Paul left (a constant question) the first community could well develop its own leadership further than at present.

"We have a different concept of what the priest is like than the official one in the church . . . . . We feel that we are as responsible for spreading the gospel as the priest is, that he is not above us but that he is with us, and we are in a circle. It is not as if he is the be-all and end-all, another kind of being who really does all the teaching and is the only one responsible for it. (Comparison was made with the other Paul, St. Paul — when the community is mature, the pastor can go on to other things).

"Paul has to connect this community of Machstrasse to the whole church. The priest is the connecting member by celebrating the eucharist. Also he would have to say 'No!' if any one of our communities said 'There is no Trinity' or such — he is responsible for good doctrine too. But only on such a basic issue will he have to stand up against the community . . . . . and must do so because the community is not on its own but it belongs to the whole church. The chief reason why most of the clergy who are not familiar with community life and have never been in such a community are against it is, first, that they are afraid of losing their important position and, second, that they fear losing their identity if the lay people do everything that they can do."

M. Vigli, Rome: "I am a layman . . . . . Until recently, lay people committed to the building up of the church have thereby been committed simply to being obedient. Those who did not obey either left the church or were marginalised by the church. The difference with the advent of basic christian communities is that laymen have remained within the basic church and yet have taken up adult responsibilities for being church. This marked a clear break with the antique tradition in which lay people accepted domestication — now, publicly, they insist on carrying their responsibilities.

"All this started in 1968 as part of a total struggle against authoritarianism both in state and church. It began as a protest against the compromise of the church with the economic political powers of society, and had a pastoral basis rather than offering a theoretical challenge to the church's doctrine or ideology."

Juan Garcia Nieto, Barcelona b.c.cs.: (On seven months spent in prison in 1969 during the Franco regime). "When I was away (and I was the only priest here during that time) the committee grew up without any priest at all. . . . . . That was a most important thing. When they did not have any priest at all, they considered themselves much more responsible and they founded the community. So when I came back I found the community completely established. (Yet often) . . . the most important communities have grown up in the institutional church because of a priest."

Theo Buss, Gospel Community, Neuchatel: "This is not a community with a very fixed membership; it's an open place where people come and go . . . . . It has not a membership by card or appointment . . . . . It's a place where people come to get nurtured, to receive the joy of communion, of community, of friendship, of being together — with which to go back to their weekly work . . . . . It's a spring of life for all, allowing us to share once a week our concerns, our intercessions."

Villeurbanne b.c.c., Lyon: "People were always coming and going, entering the community and then moving to some other part of the city or other city. But then when they moved they started other groups."

(A similar testimony came from Bordeaux)

While the b.c.cs. know themselves to be church, — not alternative church or parallel church — they do not

61

want to cut themselves off from other forms of church. It is the renewal of the total church in all its forms that they seek.

Oporto b.c.cs.: Q: Is it your aim to form an alternative church?

A: "By no means. We want to follow the way of liberation and to be with the poor. What we are against is the 'church of power'. We want to live so as to make discoveries of the church as it was meant to be. But we do this hoping for relationship and dialogue with the institutional church, so that we might share our insights with one another in one church as we journey.

"We would like to search with the official church for forms of institutionalizing which are liberating rather than constricting, and not top heavy.

"The fear of getting out of line means that there are b.c.cs. in Portugal who do not even want to get in touch with others. But if we are to move effectively we need to move together, that is to co-ordinate — which means finding some form of light institutionalizing . . . . . "

Juan Garcia Nieto, Barcelona b.c.cs.: (On some parishes' having organised themselves as b.c.cs.): "We don't claim to be an alternative church because we don't accept that we are the only church; but we want to be a voice inside, a critical voice inside the church, and we have the right to be heard in the church and we want to change the church."

Padeao de Legua b.c.c., Oporto: ". . . . . We have made several attempts to liaise with the bishop and the official structures. We will go on trying. But we get cold-shouldered."

Livorno b.c.cs.: "People who were on the move in the institutional church were excluded by the bishop: 'If bishops had been more open and less fearful, the whole movement could have had a different character.'

"Many people have been alienated from the official church, not because they have lost faith, but because they are looking for something more than that church is offering, with its fixed routines and religious practices."

Italian priest-workers: "Over these fifteen years of our existence, the gospel of Christ has been opened to the poor as it was meant to be. This has bought trouble with the hierarchy and the institutional church — not just because of the social and political activity we engage in, but our opening up of the Bible so that the place of the poor can be seen and the voice of the poor can be heard.

"I must tell you that to work with your hands alongside other people not only changes your political point of view but your religious point of view. It is very important that when the priesthood in Italy in the traditional church is so linked with the provision of money — money for masses, money for preaching, money for celebrating the sacraments — there should be priests who are free of that basis for their service. We are trying to make a change possible.

"We do not cut ourselves off from the traditional church, but rather seek contact in dialogue with parish priests — I served some seven years as a parish priest myself."

Teestubegemeinde, Wurzburg: (about priests presiding): ". . . . . I think it is a bit more difficult in the institutional church because it's just so much bigger and changes occur so much slower than those changes can occur here in our community. For me it is also important to have both the Teestubegemeinde and also the institutional church, and I myself am still involved in the church of my parish."

Oregina b.c.c., Genoa: "While remaining open to other churches, our concern is to bring our own church, the Catholic Church, to a true christian experience."

(In 1971 they were excluded by the bishop): "The square became our church. In this way we were able to give clear expression of our life together — the mass, debates, baptisms, marriages — the liturgical and sacramental life of the community.

"People came for the sacraments, for baptism, for marriage in a search for reality in worship. Quite a number of lay people and priests in this area have been affected and are trying to make different approaches. But they are a bit like Nicodemus — they feel they cannot come out in the open at this point. Besides this, there are those who know a church which negotiates concordats, and cannot believe there is another kind of church!

"At a practical level, almost all of us have remained friends with those whom we were with in the parish church, but a very small number take part in the life of the parish.

"We seek not to be a sect, but to be leaven. Our concern is that all people be confronted with the gospel."

Basque b.c.cs.: "The official church tried to call this movement a parallel church, whereas it was simply church. The gospel is more likely to make us fear the temptations of power then the possibilities of revolution."

(Concerning members of the hierarchy): "We acknowledge them to be church but insist that we are also church. If you are in the power structures, you are gravely tempted to do nothing very much. The hierarchy accuse the b.c.cs. of prompting the idea of class, and are unwilling to see that they support class structure themselves. They make no option for the poor; and say that it is the spirit that matters, when material things are inadequately provided for the poor. If this fails, they try to get at them through the structures — by relocating a priest, for instance."

Emmaus b.c.c., nr. Turin: "We do not want to develop a

hierarchy, so we make decisions about what has to be done in common. Then, according to people's different gifts, the decisions are sorted into particular tasks. People in the area keep asking who our leader is and we keep insisting that we do not have a leader. In the history of the group, wherever the community has tried to adopt a traditional leadership pattern, it has gone back. When people have struggled through to decisions they have made in common, the community has grown and matured."

Q: What happens when you cannot come to an agreed decision?

A: "We keep talking through until we come to an agreed decision!"

Q: What if you are honestly divided and cannot come to a common mind?

A: "Well, we just have time to go away and think things through again . . . . . Why should it not be humanly possible to have the kind of unity in a community which allows a common mind to develop and common decisions to be made? There is a difference between unity and uniformity. Each of us has a measure of independence. We are not made in the same mould. But we are, by choice, journeying together!"

Vomero b.c.c., Naples: "Our life is, as it were, 'managed from below'. In the old church we had no share. Our baptismal service emphasises the responsibility of the community.

"Decisions are taken according to the mind of the majority. Priests are often in the minority. Everyone has an equal say in making choices. In working towards this, members become more vividly aware of the different gifts each one has and the need to respect and give expression to the charisma of each."

In the communities, the ordained and theological professionals find a new place which relates them organically to the rest of the members in true New Testament fashion, and gives them a fresh creative role.

Emmaus b.c.c., nr. Turin: Franco (a priest): "It matters to me that I find here people creating an alternative space in which a new life can be developed. As a sign for the church, we have people of different ages and stages in their life of faith, and they can all belong to the community without being separated off. There is no separation, as in the institutional church, between priests, religious, lay people etc. − every person has gifts which are used to build up the community."

Vomero b.c.c., Naples: "All of us have become much more vividly aware of the different gifts that each has, and the need to respect and give expression to the charisma of each. Priests are not valued simply for their priesthood but for who they are, as persons. The group's theology of the priesthood has changed in light of the realisation that everyone has gifts to contribute.

Everyone shares in a priesthood.

"If a priest were to die or to leave it would depend on the maturity and the autonomy of the group whether it just continued or not. Some groups might be strong, some too frail to continue . . . . . Actually in the community of the resurrection in Florence, ten years ago, the priest died. The community simply continued. Before the priest died they had experimented with eucharistic services in which the priest was not celebrant, so they were not priest-dependant . . . . . In similar circumstances, b.c.cs. in the south of Italy had died. In the south of Italy the cultural and sociological catholic conditioning has been so strong that, where priests have been withdrawn, groups have died. Lay strength was simply not sufficiently developed yet . . . . "

"The animator must not take over the position of leader as it is traditionally thought of. She or he must emerge from the group as someone having their confidence. The position must be a temporary one and the person acting this way must be ready to give place to someone else . . . . .

". . . . . In one sense, the authority lies in a person who has the capacity to unite a group and keep it alive; but it is the group that recognises this authority and gives its weight. The charisma of a particular person does not come from the community but is a gift of God: the community and ministry within it is sacramental."

Frankfurt, in general comment: (Concerning their two experts in exegesis). "Most of the time they encouraged us to speak with one another. Sure, they were ahead of us — but they never looked down on us so as to make us silent. (One priest presided. After five years he went elsewhere.)

Q: When they left, did they leave a very big gap?

A: "At first we thought there was a very big gap, but I don't think it really did turn out so. Sometimes I thought it was like the apostles after the death of Jesus. I know the picture seems an exaggeration; but it was genuinely a feeling like that that we experienced. After a time we gathered again and moved on. We think of these two now in a very friendly and thankful way. But we don't need them any more. We are clear about that."

Q: Do you feel that a charismatic leader is one of the main starting points for these groups?

A: "Yes, I do. I think this is very important. Of course it's very dangerous at the same time — since most people could become dependent on someone like that, and this dependence is partly just laziness. When someone is there who develops things very well, it is very easy to let that person go ahead."

Nico Roozen, Utrecht b.c.cs.: "The community is now the subject of the liturgy and takes responsibility for the development and for contributions to it; and the priest and pastor have found a new place at the heart of the community instead of over it."

Endrestrasse b.c.c., Vienna: "Every second month we have a review, as a total community, of the life of the community and the way it is developing its agenda. In that kind of meeting, Fr. Mueller has no more right to speak than anyone else. If he has some ideas, they can be accepted or rejected just as the ideas of any lay person could be accepted or rejected by the total community. So the old barrier between priest and laity is really broken down in this community."

Vomero b.c.c., Naples: concerning the b.c.c.: "They are now clear that to have celibacy as a calling may be important for the life of the church, but to have it as a law for the ordained is wrong.

"In the institutional church, the priest is among the people in sacramental and bureaucratic terms. In the b.c.cs., the priest or whoever gives leadership, is among them in terms of equality and fraternity. The whole community has a sacramental value, the priesthood within it."

La Traboule b.c.c., Lyon: "Married priests in b.c.cs. are 'catalysts without dominating', while those attached to parishes have hardly changed at all. Their distinctive role is to represent the link with the whole church."

Coteto b.c.c., Livorno: "Priests play an important part in b.c.c. development — with the dominance of the Roman Catholic church in Italian culture, lay people have difficulty in shaking themselves clear of assumptions of a hierarchical church. Priests who take a new way encourage confidence in others who seek new ways."

Schwechet b.c.c., Vienna (re the Priest): "He gives the impulses of christian life, of spirituality, and he is the link with the universal church; but concerning the life of the community he is one of us, he is really a man for team-work."

Trout, Machtrasse b.c.c., Vienna: "It's not just Paul (the priest) giving new directions and new ways of thinking about things to us, but a lot of ideas coming from ourselves as well . . . . . The spirit of the community is much more like the Brazilian ones with everyone on the same level. Of course, Paul is an important factor in it, but I don't think it would make a really serious difference any more in the community if he weren't there . . . . . At the moment I think that if Paul wouldn't be there, the community would go further."

A prophetic observation:

Padeao da legua b.c.c., Oporto: " . . . . . I got a fresh awareness of peoples' gifts and responsibilities . . . . . what came home to me astonishingly was the fact that I was church!

"The b.c.cs. won't die. At present one of their great weaknesses is that while they develop sporadic liaison, they lack real co-ordination. We must not worry about our differences — they come largely from the different situations and histories we

66

have inherited. Deep down the Portuguese b.c.cs. realise that they are on the same road, facing common problems, sharing common joys: and their differences are an enrichment of one another.

"Portuguese b.c.cs. have had an exodus, but need to go through the desert. At present they are not mature enough for combating the pressures on them by church and society. They have to learn to persevere and get stronger. Those which are part of parish structures have to develop more definitely as b.c.cs. — otherwise what happens is that, when an 'open' priest is replaced, the work stops . . . . "

THE DEVELOPMENT OF COUNTERSIGNS – SOME EXPERIENCES

LIFESTYLE – PORTUGESE COMMUNITIES

From a visit by Margaret and Ian Fraser

Natalie led us across the high span of the Dom Luis I bridge over the Douro to the main part of the city of Oporto. The crags we faced were topped by the magnificent Archbishop's palace which, though now used as offices, speaks still of the lordly power which the church once exercised, and reminds us of the extent to which that ecclesiastical power is still in evidence. We reached the other end of the bridge and she gestured downwards. At the foot of the palace lay the dwellings of the poor, with cramped quarters, broken roofs.

"Every day" said Natalie "there is set out before the eyes of the people of this city this visible sign of what the church stands for. What wonder then, that we have been called to contradict that sign and to live a countersign."

The countersign is the style of life of basic christian communities in Oporto. They are small in number. They look frail. They are pregnant with the future.

Pregnant with the future? Sometimes we, their guests, had to shake ourselves to make sure that we were not back in the first century. The apostles' teaching, the fellowship, the breaking of bread, the prayers; the holding of everything in common and the distribution of possessions as the need of each required; the breaking of bread in private houses and the sharing of meals with unaffected joy – for us these became a living experience.

With a sophistication open only to those who respond to the good news with directness and unaffected generosity, the b.c.cs. in Oporto have developed styles of life which express, in the complexities of our contemporary societies, essential features of the early church.

Members share their personal lives with great openness, offering honest criticism when it is called for, sustaining one another in the ups and downs, maintaining warm, committed relationships.

They share food. Sometimes they go to a house where it is provided, sometimes they bring contributions and prepare a common meal.

Is someone put out of work or faced with some other emergency? The crisis will be made the concern of the whole community. Help will be given at once and, when the meeting takes place at which continuing need is assessed, the new situation will be taken into account and the whole community will be prepared to live at a lower level to ensure that a member's reduced circumstances are taken care of. In a poor community ('we are basic earners, there are no bourgeois among us') money can still be found for Justice and Peace and Third World causes, and solidarity is established with marginalised people at home and abroad.

Homes are shared. The first time it happened we were caught out without so much as a toothbrush between us (but no problem - nightclothes and other small accessories are also made available). Is something happening in this part of Oporto or that other town in Costa Verde? Then people gather there, work into the night. Those whose homes are within easy reach, duly leave. Others use a spare bed or a sofa or make a shakedown on the floor. The house, who ever owns it, becomes visibly the house of the community. At one point we let it be known that we wanted to do some work on documentation we had gathered. No problem. A member offered us her one-bedroom flat (no bed there — but a mattress on the floor) and went to live with another member so that we could use the time available to the best advantage. Manuela is accustomed to lifting the phone in her office and hearing something such as the following: "We are using your place for a few days, but we'll leave a space for you". Keys are distributed around. Those who drop by just for a rest or to cook a meal do not even feel the need to tell Manuela they have used her premises.

Even at the bus stops, the one who has tickets uses them for the whole company.

All this is done in a framework of great realism, with ready acceptance that there will be a variety of styles and standards of life among the membership. The house of Lena, Manuel and Anna is large enough to take extra people comfortably and is well furnished. Natalie's damp little cabin has three rooms but it is no bigger than a modest-sized caravan — three people would crowd its space. There is no effort at producing uniformity. There is a genuine fellowship of sharing.

Spiritual athletes, these? Anything but. Listen to them when, the elements duly consecrated, the bread broken and the wine poured out, they tell of their own brokenness and pour out their hearts in union with the bread and wine. You will hear of frustration and failure in relationships affecting husbands, wives, young people, parents. You will be told of illnesses and despondencies. There will be word of humiliations and stresses at work, in searching for work, and looking for alternative work.

"Cast down, but not destroyed": the words come

instinctively to mind. The theme for the day is "How are we to live the joy of our faith?" The sorrows shared form the context within which varied testimonies are made to a power which overcomes in and through suffering. Isabel, tears streaming down her cheeks from the remembered vexation of being blamed by her employers for taking a week off work on doctor's orders to calm a suspected ulcer*, brightens. Her face becomes sun shining through rain. She ends, with quiet firmness "We fight on".

Members of the community do not depart until they have consolidated plans for the political and social engagements to which faith directs them. Members must run risks equivalent to that of stoning, which Stephen faced when he spoke of God taking a hand in the whole process of history now summed up in Christ; risks equivalent to that of being hauled before magistrates which Peter and John soon found was the reward for preaching such a Christ.

* Isabel died of cancer within the year.

ST. PAUL'S OUTSIDE THE WALLS —
A BASIC CHRISTIAN COMMUNITY IN ROME

On March 3rd, 1964, the Chapter of the Benedictine Monks of the Abbey of St. Paul's Basilica Outside the Walls elected as their Abbot Giovanni Battista Franzoni. He was 36 at the time and St. Paul's was an important bishop's residence and an extra-territorial possession of the Vatican State. In his mid-30's Franzoni became a member of the Italian Bishops' Conference and the youngest voting member of the second Vatican Council.

Following the Council, Franzoni began 'Pauline Studies' inviting Protestant scholars to join Roman Catholics in these.

To his own people, he presented the view of the function of an abbey which he summarised in an interview later on:

"In a crisis such as this, which is shaking our entire culture, I and a group of monks near to me thought that a Benedictine Abbey had to discover its role in the social transformations taking place. We had predecessors in history. In the dramatic epoch of the passage from Roman culture to that of the High-middle Ages, we saw that the abbeys had had different roles, and not simply that of conservation but roles of 'witness', of being concrete ferments of christian newness in the world. The abbeys had always had contact with and taken initiatives in favour of the people who lived around them.

"In Italy they founded agricultural co-operatives in the ninth century, one thousand one hundred years ago and right in the middle of the crisis of the barbaric age. The co-operatives bore social fruit which is still recogniseable in Nonnantola and around Modena. In Germany they founded artisan schools which became proud and large commercial centres.

"Then something stopped all this. Now we have lost the original and real meaning of the abbeys.

"What had happened was that some works which were connected with and determined by different historical and environmental circumstances were crystalised and considered to be 'the institution'. There was a lack of understanding that the abbey had been a place which opened itself to the persons who lived around it, without imposing its own choices."

He went on to reflect:

"We asked ourselves what a Benedictine Abbey meant in a densely populated, urban neighbourhood."

In 1968 he started a 'Saturday evening assembly' which centred on the Bible readings which were to be the basis for preaching on the Sunday. There was an attempt to see how the biblical message addressed itself to the issues of the day. The small group gathered around the Word of God grew to about 200 persons and the Sunday service attracted an average attendance of about 2,000 people. A community came into being which was wrestling to relate the faith to life. In May 1970 they drafted a letter sent to the President of the Italian Republic in which they asked that 'the holiday in honour of the republic (June 2nd) no longer be celebrated by an expensive and anti-educational military parade.' This intervention was a scandal in its time, going against the 'non-political' support and use by the Roman Catholic Church of the 'Catholic' political party. Meantime the Corpus Domini procession of the Basilica had been transformed so that its themes helped people to grapple with the burning concerns of their time. In 1971 the theme was 'Political Engagement in the City' and in 1972 'To Be Church'. In 1971 the basic christian community movement, initially covering 40 communities, developed a national organisation. The community declared themselves ready for 'a prophetic method of struggle and of civil disobedience to create an alternative society to the present one' and this meant action 'against church structures which offer support and political cover to violent and authoritarian regimes and to governments which accept the militaristic logic'.

On March 20th, 1971, 200 members of the St. Paul's Basilica Community discussed the occupation of a nearby factory, the Crespi. They went into the pros and cons to find what the gospel required. They were mainly students and white-collar workers, including managers in industry and employees of the state television company. There were a few unemployed and blue-collar workers. Against the grain of their own self-interest, middle-class christians interpreted the gospel to mean a decision to support publicly the Crespi workers. A few days later, the community co-occupied another factory in that area, joining the workers of Aerostatica.

The Vatican became alarmed. It found it impossible to establish any legal or doctrinal basis for getting rid of Franzoni; but, in spite of the acknowledged autonomy which the Benedictines are meant to enjoy, it burrowed its way in. After Franzoni's best-seller pastoral letter *The Earth is God's* (over 100,000 copies sold and translations made in French, Spanish and English), he was given the option of stopping such publications, or resigning. What touched the Vatican nerve was the way he applied biblical research to the immediate situation, especially the documenting and exposure of Vatican finance and that of religious orders in real estate speculation which made the condition of the poor even worse. He was squeezed out, and he and the community took over a nearby warehouse as a base for worship and action.

In the post-Vatican period the date 1968 is very important. The conservative backlash to Vatican II was gaining ground and the forces for change were coming to a head. In September, 1968, Catholic university students occupied the city's cathedral in Parma to denounce the involvement of church authorities in economic and political power structures and to insist on the right of lay people to be the church. The police were called in and ended the occupation, which the Pope publicly condemned. It looked as if some hope still existed for the new, prophetic voices because, on February 4th 1974, a diocesan convention on the 'Ills of Rome' was organised by Cardinal Ugo Poletti. No barrier was raised against the participation of the basic christian communities in Rome. These worked hard in preparation, and formulated documents with biblical-prophetic perceptions which were mostly approved by the diocesan assembly. Later that year, however, the referendum on civil divorce was to produce even deeper cleavage. Franzoni at first refused to speak. But then, in late February, the Italian Bishops' Conference declared that all Roman Catholics were obliged in conscience to vote against the state's freedom to permit civil divorce. Franzoni's April publication *My Kingdom is not of this World* was a response, attacking 'integralism' (the idea that authorities can logically deduce from the faith political options for the faithful to take) and took his stand thus:

"Christ did not intend truth as an ideology but as a light, a ferment, as salt which exercises its action . . . . . by placing itself in the midst of the social-historical context . . . . . for the church must preach to all nations."

On April 27th, Franzoni suffered *'suspensio a divinis'*. Over 300 priests signed a document of solidarity with Franzoni in which they not only defended his personal integrity and his theological position but stated that the attitude of the Italian Bishops' Conference was a "serious repression of the most elementary freedoms and a clear negation of the spirit of the gospel and of Vatican II". Oddly, he was told that the suspension would be lifted if he left the country !

During the Week of Prayer for Christian Unity in January 1975, the community sent a donation to W.C.C.'s Programme to Combat Racism, "We believe that the WCC programme to combat racism", the community explained in an attached letter, "is a step into the social arena of justice in which there can be no credal division of the one Lord, Jesus Christ, and thus, is a step toward the ecumenical unity which we all desire.

"Indeed. the question of Christian unity is very complex, but we of St. Paul's community are convinced that if we do not work together for the concrete liberation of humanity, we will never be able to establish that unity of Christians which Jesus of Nazareth desires . . . . . The WCC's project is for this reason all the more a sign of hope to us as believers in that it encourages us to protest whenever and wherever we see one person or group of people exploit others. It also encourages us never to let the·exploiter act or pretend to act as though he has received the silent blessing of the disciples of Christ to rule over his brothers and sisters and to oppress them."

After this, Franzoni deliberately drew more into the background of the community so that a variety of other kinds of leadership could emerge.

On July 31st, 1976, Franzoni was unfrocked, elevated to the lay state. These actions went clean against official procedure. No doctrinal errors were ever identified and there was no theological trial such as had been guaranteed by Pope Paul VI. Bishop Bettazzi reacting to the unfrocking, wrote: "I am surprised over certain accusations against your orthodoxy in that I have known your soundness in the faith, your familiarity with the Word of God and your love of the church".

In 1976 the St. Paul's community was excluded from the Italian Bishops' Conference Convention on 'Evangelisation and Human Advancement' but it sent to the convention a 55 page open letter on *Violence in the City and in the Church of Rome.* It spoke about "a very subtle and insidious violence which the dominant class exercises on the religious, ideological and cultural level, aimed at influencing and conditioning the institutions that produce and spread culture" especially schools, universities and churches. "This type of violence is carried out in various forms. It places value on consumerism and confuses 'being' with 'having' so as to defend the market which increases the value of money. It creates a mirage of freedom . . ." and as a result "the value of one's private possession (property) becomes the principal measure to judge personal realisation and self affirmation. And this illusory, or at the most marginal freedom, exalts the myth of being well-off and personal egoism blocks the recognition of a common condition of exploitation and of oppression and impedes the search for unity and the development of a collective conscience."

Ed Grace, editor of *The Bridge* observed of this unlikely community which was criticising, on a gospel basis, society "These relatively well-to-do Romans did not turn aside nor try to water down the Word of God, and the resulting tensions and contradictions created a form of liberating energy." He went on "the Word of God among socially comfortable people is not a symbol of security but a two-edged sword which cuts simultaneously through their economic and material well-being (their flesh) and their cultural, ideological and psychological defences (their consciences). Many highly educated people in protected situations found themselves called to apply their trained minds on behalf of the marginalised in society. They researched, exposed causes, denounced the reality, proposed alternatives, mobilised acts of repentance, protestation, and the building of just structures."

Trained minds were bent to the work of analysis, communicators amplified the voice of the oppressed through journalistic and radio skills, the economically privileged

74

supported smaller and pressured communities.

Some points about St. Paul's general assembly:

Every one has equal voice and equal rights to speak. Consensus, not majority vote, is the means of decision-making. A minority is not overborne; rather more consideration will be given. This stimulates the growth of members at various speeds without minorities being marginalised and it gives time for insights to develop.

If a 'mind of the people' is not reached, sessions will continue until there is some agreed conclusion. This happened when Franzoni was laicised. The community debated whether to hold eucharist without the ordained person presiding; in the end, since a minority still felt the need for an ordained person, that practice continued at least at that stage.

The warehouse premises are put at the service of a substantial number of organisations in the neighbourhood.

The large Saturday evening assembly for Bible study was making too many of those present voiceless, so there was a breakdown into smaller groups. 'Each Bible group is responsible on a rotating basis for the preparation of the Sunday eucharist service which includes choosing the hymns and writing or selecting the eucharistic prayer (said by the whole community) and above all giving the homily (preaching) which as often as not is done by a lay woman. This prepared homiletic phase always precedes the collective spontaneous preaching and witness during which all can come forward to comment on the text, to say a prayer, bring testimony, share a problem or a joy. And, while being polemical about preceding textual interpretations is strictly forbidden in practice, it sometimes happens that a variety of contradictory or at least dialectical interpretations are presented. It should be noted that this form of preaching is usually extremely instructive for the members of the community, providing deep insights and well-rounded perspectives.'

Approximately 80% of the community are active in trade unions, political parties, or non-party social action initiatives.

The committee on the 'Constitutional Rights of the Handicapped and/or Invalid Citizens' does not have the label 'christian' in spite of the large basis of christian membership.

The children's group, 40 to 50 children and adults together, carry out research on issues which they choose and periodically develop the eucharistic service, deciding on the theme, doing the preaching etc.

Interview with
FR. JUAN-GARCIA NIETO,
Barcelona, 1980

IMF: Juan Garcia, when we went to San Martin (where the community which works in four different groups in this area was meeting for the Saturday and the Sunday) the first thing that I noticed was flowers. I believe that the children (and this would show the place that they had in the community) gathered wild flowers, and when people arrived they gave them a bunch. Is that right? Is it just a gesture from the children of kindness and thoughtfulness? They were the hosts of the gathering!

JGN: Yes, that's a thing that usually we do; because we look forward to having this as a meeting-with-festivity. We want the children to get involved in our meeting — although we know that in our serious discussions they can't take part. Also usually (today and yesterday it was not possible) we have a eucharist also with them. Today we just left them at the swimming pool to have fun. But we want them to be conscious that they are members of the community although they don't understand all that goes on. We ask them to greet people when they come, giving them flowers, acting as hosts to the others.

IMF: You mean that in the eucharist or Mass they usually partake as well — or are they just present?

JGN: They are present; and sometimes we have organised a special eucharist for them with songs and with a special type of explanation of the Bible and the Gospel suited to their mentality.

IMF: And do they partake?

JGN: They partake, yes.

IMF: The next thing which struck me was that a whole part of the evening was given just to children's play, adults playing with the children and the children playing by themselves. Again I felt there was an emphasis that the community is not just of adults but is a total community.

JGN: Yes. Formerly we had an experience that was not good enough: that we go to this place and we, the adult people have our meetings and we leave the children without any participation. The inclusive type of gathering we now have happens three or four times per year. We go away to the country. We want these meetings to be a kind of celebration (we say in Spanish *con vivencia*) with families, with children. We don't want them to meet 'outside their own interests', we want them to participate. So yesterday we preferred to stay the whole afternoon with them. Then we had our meeting once they went to bed.

IMF: The meeting of the community took place — that is the adults in the community — when the children had gone to bed. You spoke for quite a long time. There was plenty of sharing the next day, but not that evening. Why?

JGN: Since, for the last three months I had the opportunity to meet different communities all around Spain, in the north, in the south, in Andalusia, they wanted me to share with them my own experience and a summary of the things I heard. Since also the theme of today was the new values in our new society and the things we were discussing in our meetings all around Spain concerned the same problem, they wanted me to give the summary so that they had some broader canvas to work against next morning. But usually we never start with a long talk. We start immediately with meetings of little groups as we did this morning.

IMF: Could you just select some of the points that you found important when you visited these other groups — maybe similarities with the group development here in the Barcelona area, maybe some different fresh and challenging ways in which other groups are moving?

JGN: We need to note more or less the differences of these groups. Two months ago I was with a variety of communities in a gathering of grassroots communities at the centre of Andalusia. Most of the people were countrymen, they were not from urban areas but had a very uncomplicated approach to life.

IMF: Peasants and others from rural areas?

JGN: Yes, rural areas in Andalusia, with very tough problems because they have no work; and the poverty in that part of Spain is frightening.

IMF: Do they own their own land?

JGN: No, they never own their own land. They work for the landowners.

IMF: So they are really land-workers, not small farmers.

JGN: That's right. Some of them belong to a co-operative movement, because the co-operative movement is getting very strong in the south of Spain now in some places — mainly in that place I was in, Antequera, and near Malaga, not on the coast, but inland.

IMF: And what kind of development of life did you find there?

JGN: Well, it surprised me very much. I found they, in their types of communities, had a great preoccupation with a new reading of the Bible and of the gospel. I would say most of them belonged to peasant movements, rural trade unions; they are politically engaged in the communist party or in the socialist party. They involve people in politics, in the peasants' struggle. That was very interesting for me. I knew them, because I have been there at other times — because most of the people who are in our own community come from that area of Spain. They are immigrants in Barcelona. Those who have come here were very interested in how these communities were developing because when these people here left Andalusia 15 years ago, they didn't know about this new type of church at all. They used to belong to a very traditional way of life. Now they have discovered this new type of church here. They are very much impressed that in the last ten years in their 'home' area all these new communities have developed as well.

IMF: So, this was landless people, who were already politicised, and now in addition to their political awareness, were concentrating on the insights the Bible could give them?

JGN: Yes, and as we would put it in our own words, on building a new type of church in the country and co-ordinating with others in the Comunidades Populares of Spain. That tie-up was one of the experiences I had in the last three months.

IMF: Did they centre themselves on the eucharist? They were biblically based, they were politically active — did the priests acknowledge them and were they with them at the eucharist, or did the structured church view them in a fairly hostile way?

JGN: The priests of these villages are very open-minded; and these communities are more or less, I wouldn't say led by them, but supported by them. The Bishop of Malaga is one of the open-minded bishops that we have in Spain. He is a Catalan bishop who had been a bishop in Latin America. He is now in Malaga and he is not against the movement of Comunidades Populares, but quite the contrary. Although he is engaged in the 'holy structure' he is quite in the line of Bishop Cassal Valiga, his good friend in Brazil. He had been also in Chile during the time of Allende. He was then a priest and when he came back to Spain he was made bishop.

IMF: It seems to me to be true that the growth of the communities of the people depends very largely on the release of gifts of lay people which have been hidden and unused before. But it also seems quite characteristic that you have a priest, or a religious, or a pastor, or someone like that who is giving support; and the main difference is that instead of their being over the people they are alongside the people, they are with the people. It just suddenly struck me today that this means priests, instead of being like the shepherds in the Old Testament who were to rule and control the flocks, being much more like Jesus who said 'Now you will have to get on with it, but I will be with you'. In some French basic communities there is always a priest at the eucharist, but if you came in you wouldn't know who was the priest because the presiding is done by the people together. But the priest is there and they think it important to have the priest there. Is that fairly common? Are there many communities that are of lay people only, or is there usually a priest or a pastor?

JGN: I would say that there is usually a priest in the

community, but as you were saying he never takes a place of control over the community. For instance, as you saw this morning, the man who was reading the lesson is a married man and is not a priest. Sometimes a young lady does that part. We priests are there, and we participate. Yet it is also true that, perhaps because of our work we have sometimes to be absent. Then they meet and they celebrate the eucharist without any priest at all — those people you were with today.

IMF: So as Schillebeeck says, the Mass or the eucharist is the people's work — well it was until the 11th or 12th century; and 'This is my body' means also 'This is the body of Christ gathered.' And when you preside you are representing that body?

JGN: Yes. That's the type of celebration we have each week.

IMF: What other visits were you sharing with the people?

JGN: I was in the north of Spain, in Santander, just four weeks ago, and we had a meeting of four or five Comunidades Populares and Christians for Socialism because they are more or less on the same lines. Not all Comunidades Populares take the direction of the Christians for Socialism, but in the area in Santander they certainly do. We spent two days together, as today; we were in a house in the country Saturday and Sunday mainly discussing the problem of hope and the possibilities for hope and the possibilities for disenchantment, and most of the things I said yesterday were the resumé of things I heard from people there.

IMF: You talked very interestingly of the characteristics of the life of the people who work on the land. What were the characteristics in the Santander area?

JGN: Well, they are industrial people who work in big industries in the north of Spain.

IMF: And what difference do you note in their kind of groups?

JGN: I would say the difference is the type of political engagement. Regarding the type of reflection . . . . . I wouldn't say it is more intellectual but certainly it represents a more culturally influenced approach to problems because they belong to an urban society.

IMF: The problems are more complex?

JGN: For instance, in the meeting in Santander we were discussing the compatibility between Marxism and Christianity, something which was not a concern in Andalusia. Certainly there they have more ideological problems; it was a different level of culture, I would say; yet in the end the problems were the same in essence.

IMF: Would you say then that they had a kind of three-cornered thing; that they had the biblical involvement, they had the political analysis, but they also had an attempt to discover the shape of a different society?

JGN: Yes, but with more difficulties. In Andalusia there was more poverty, but there was also this new type of work through the co-operative movement. In the northern part of Spain, an industrial area, they don't see an immediate solution towards a new type of society, though they certainly see the need to fight. There was a very interesting discussion there between a group who were arguing 'We do not have to work inside the political parties. We have enough with our spiritual fraternity.' But the majority were saying 'That's not enough. The spiritual is a very important element, it is part of our life, it is a kind of inspiration; but we have to go through what we call "historical mediations", through political parties, trade union activities and so on.' These latter were people who were engaged mostly either in the Communist Party or in the Socialist Party.

IMF: Is there a greater variety of involvement now? Are there some, for instance, who are pressing much more for change in the social sphere, in the sphere of local community development, and not so much within the parties for larger concerns?

JGN: There is a bigger variety in this Barcelona group. We have people here who are town councillors.

IMF: So some concentrate on local politics?

JGN: Yes, local politics. Others are concentrating on industrial politics, on trade union activities, on political parties. There are others, perhaps 50%, who are concentrating on cultural activities. Cultural activities embrace not only teaching in the schools here in our district but also what we call here in our town 'People's schools'. This is mainly for adult education; and we organise through these People's Schools different types of talks on history, urban problems, medical problems — for families, for the mothers; and we also do classical and popular music.

IMF: And is it basically adult education to extend people's horizons, or has it an element of conscientisation?

JGN: Certainly it has conscientisation in it because all the problems faced in adult education here follow more or less along the lines of Paolo Freire; people in the community are working in that style. So we have a very great variety of forms of engagement here.

IMF: So, it really is the pressure for 'cultural freedom', as Paolo would put it, that people are after in their cultural involvement.

JGN: It is in that sense that we understand it, yes.

IMF: In relation to the last group we mentioned, why is it that some christians are committing themselves rather to the Christians for Socialism movement? Is it because some of them feel that to shape out a quite new society is what matters, and are they prepared to break down the old one? What does the involvement of christians in that movement mean?

JGN: It means a very simple thing. First of all, it does not mean that the Christians for Socialism are presenting a political proposal for a specific type of society. The main issues or the main objectives of Christians for Socialism are three, I would say, as we understand them here: First to help christians of our communities to understand that to change our society we have to change it through historical movements, not christian movements maybe but movements worked out by the people. I mean trade unions and political parties fighting for socialism. We don't have any political power. But we understand that to accept the gospel is to accept a type of society fought for already since many years ago by political parties, by trade unions, by people. So Christians for Socialism would act to help christians to understand that; and help them not to be afraid to consider themselves Marxist; and help them understand what it means to be in the class struggle, what it means to be an allied company using Marxist theory. The second objective is to build up a people's church through basic communities and to have a new reading of the Bible. Thirdly, I would add, to make people of our country understand that to be a christian does not mean to be a man of the right as it was understood during Franco's time and previously, when to be a christian meant to be a man of the right. These would be mainly the aims of Christians for Socialism.

IMF: And is it anti-capitalistic?

JGN: By definition so.

IMF: Now you happened to mention Franco. I thought I got from just one or two hints that it was a hard and difficult struggle to start what has become people's communities, because they did start during Franco's time and the police would have been very hard on that: am I right?

JGN: Yes, that's right. We knew each other here in our district, and we decided in 1968 to start a new type of community. At that time, 12 years ago, in Spain there were no grassroots communities.

IMF: You were the first of all?

JGN: Here, yes. At the same time they were just beginning to appear. But there was not any tradition. We had heard of some experiences in Italy and in Latin America, but none at all here in our country. I remember the first time we met there were 12 of us. The police came in and they said we couldn't be around in this house because we were more people than was permitted by Franco's law. We used to meet in a school. Twice I remember the police came in and they stopped us. But at that time there were priests in the churches who were completely against the government and they gave us permission to have gatherings in the local parish premises. Some of our committee were in prison, not because of this activity but because of political and trade union activity. I was myself for 7 months in prison in 1969. I was the only priest here; and it was during that time that the community grew up, without any priest at all.

IMF: Was that important?

JGN: I think that was a **most** important thing. When they did not have any priest at all, they considered themselves much more responsible and **they** founded the community. When I came back I found the community completely established.

IMF: That's interesting, because Franzoni, when he was debarred from presiding at the Mass, then realised he had been a bit like a chieftain with his retainers around him. Once he was removed, the community testified that far more leadership came forward than previously.

JGN: It was all a very good experience for me. It gave a lesson to me not to have any type of front leadership in the community.

IMF: Do you think that the repression they suffered gave a certain character to the community?

JGN: At that time, at the end of the sixties, most christian people were engaged in politics. Until that time they had been much more afraid to belong to political parties — because of the dangers of clandestinity, and because of the prohibition by the church of christians being members of the Communist Party and so on. But they found themselves fighting in the factories and in the clandestine trade unions. One of the first issues for us was what it meant for a christian to be involved in 'atheistic' (as they said at that time) political parties, for instance the Communist Party. That was one of our main preoccupations at that time. I think the community life helped them and helped us; because the members of the community asked us priests to be engaged in the same way that they were engaged. So we became active members of trade unions and/or political parties.

IMF: So the b.c.cs. developed a style of life looking to a 'different christian way'; and you as priests, had to pick up the elements of that style of life that they had already worked out?

JGN: Yes. Also a new type of experience for us was the solidarity practised between members of the community when some of them were in prison; and with other people, friends of ours, who were not christians but were living in the same districts, in the same streets, working in the same factories: being with them in the same type of fight and with great solidarity. So many people said that at that time they discovered what christianity meant. It meant to be 'hombre solidario' as we would say today, without making any difference between christians and non-christians. I think that was the first formative step of our community. . . . .

IMF: In, I think, Holland and Belgium there are members of christian grassroots communities that belong to right wing parties. They believe that there should not be an excluding point to people who are prepared to explore what it means to be politically involved in terms of the gospel. But not in Spain?

82

JGN: Very certainly, not in Spain, because our communities are very clear that people who are in right wing political parties are people who accept capitalism and accept the way of exploitation. We found it completely impossible to be members of grassroots communities who have made a very clear statement for a new society which is not compatible with the capitalist structure, and to act otherwise. So you won't find in any grassroots communities people who belong to politically right parties.

IMF: Were the areas visited the two that you reported on or were there any others?

JGN: There are some others. I was also in a group in Madrid and Saragossa and then in Tarragona. The experiences were more or less the same as in Santander.

IMF: Once you had done this reporting people really had a ball. They went outside and first of all they had a bit of horseplay — some kind of leap-frog game where four people were the frogs, and others tried to leap as far as they could on them. Then there was a bonfire; and the local songs and dancing around the bonfire went on till Two or Three in the morning, although we left at One in the morning. This seemed to me to be very happy and spontaneous. When people decide to have that kind of gathering (in this case because of the remembrance of St. Peter with a very delicious kind of pastry and the local champagne) do they always develop the fun and games as spontaneously as that without anybody organising it? Is it the kind of community that has so much vitality in itself it just comes out whenever there is any kind of opportunity?

JGN: I would say that's the best way to do things. The most spontaneous thing is the best thing. Yes, this a very traditional feast in our country, in Catalonia, the eve of St. Peter, to have bonfires and to have these type of pastries and some beans. There is the same thing on the eve of St. John, with bonfires and so on. Also during the winter, some other meetings we hold in houses are like the evening yesterday around the fire — in winter inside the house, telling jokes and singing and so on. This is one of the things which marks our community, to have this type of festivity in a very spontaneous way.

IMF: It seemed to me that there was a kind of wholeness about this. You had serious discussions, serious talks, the playing with the children, the fun, the spontaneous fun, the eating together, the communion, and then relaxation for an hour by the swimming pool before we came back again. That was a balance that seems to have been lost by the traditional church. It is now being regained. Would you agree?

JGN: We have to manifest the faith not only saying we believe in God, we believe in Christ, we believe in people; we have to manifest it also through songs, through playing with the children, through everything which means some kind of gaiety. For instance in the last gathering of all Comunidades Populares

83

in Barcelona three months ago, half the day they just had feasts and songs and so on. There were serious discussions. But half the day was to celebrate, to sing and so on, to have this type of very happy gathering.

IMF: And then, at the end of the day, we had a single dormitory with double bunks beds, and I was really very taken by the way in which people changed clothes, got to bed, got up out of bed, without bothering too much about the fact that men and women were together. In that, the impression that came across to me was the impression that you get when it's a family. You know, if you're with strangers you're very careful not to do any stripping. But here people just turned aside a bit and changed their clothes. It seemed to me that that living for the night in the dormitory was an additional sign of the solidarity and trust that people had. Am I exaggerating?

JGN: You could be right, yes. We have known each other for many years already. For instance, some of them knew each other in the community, and then married in the community. They didn't know each other before they came to the community, and so the marriage came out of their knowing each other. Some of the families have grown up inside the community. So I think it is a type of big family. I think that it's a very spontaneous development — and we act thus even when we are with people from different communities and we don't know them. I think this type of spontaneity is always present in our relationships in the grassroots communities.

IMF: Then in the morning, people met in groups and quite clearly everybody participated in the discussions. One of the things they were fastening on, for instance, was whether you really needed to belong to the official institutional church or not. There was quite a bit of discussion about that. I find that it's very characteristic of basic christian communities in Europe that they want to stay in relationship to the institutional church, because you always have to have some form of continuity through the centuries provided by the institutional church. Its job is to give them space to develop — and to stay with them, instead of either just rejecting them and trying to snuff them out or trying to assimilate them back into its own life again. What would be the attitude of the communities in Spain in general? Would it be the same?

JGN: I would say it would be the same. There are differences. For instance, there are some communities here in Barcelona which have nothing to do with the official church. But I wouldn't say that would be the main line of the communities. For instance, the most important communities have grown up inside the institutional church because of the priest. There were, in most cases, worker priests or other people who were working. It is interesting to note that all grassroots communities are in the working-class districts, where these priests during Franco's time became very aware of what it meant to be a priest engaged in the people's interest. They developed a type of open church, not closed-minded churches.

Most of the communities meet on parish premises. Some parishes have even organised themselves as people's communities. So we don't claim to be an alternative church because we don't pretend we are the only church. But we want to be a voice inside, a critical voice inside the whole church. And we have a right to be heard in the church and we want to change the church. So for us the main line, I would say, is not to say 'We don't want to have anything to do with you.' We want rather to help them to be combative. We want all the structures of the church to lose power. We engage in the interests of people. There are different emphases in different communities; but there is a common acceptance that we are members of the church: and we want to change this church, give it a different type of structure etc.

IMF: And you think that the communities that have no kind of relationship with the official church are in danger of moving away and doing their own thing; or do you think the other communities that are related to them can keep them adequately in contact with the on-going stream of official church life?

JGN: I don't know. Concerning the experience I have had and the things I have heard of these types of communities which usually used to be near the parish churches and then go away and they hold to their own way — they usually disappear. That's my own experience.

IMF: And they should. I remember interviewing a Baptist who was leading the gathering of christian grassroots communities in Rome, and he said that if people retreat into the Bible alone or retreat into the political and social situation alone, they're better to disappear. They need to keep these two together to live the faith today.

JGN: I would say that would be the same experience here.

IMF: What were the main items of concern in your group?

JGN: The main question we tried to answer first of all was — what, at this moment of our social, cultural, political, ecclesiastical situation, it means to us to be part of a community, and what we want from the community. Secondly, what are we prepared to give to the community, and where are the new challenges in accordance with which to live a new style of life in accordance with our socialist objective to develop a change in the values we live by.

We were not discussing 'churches' and 'communities'. We were mainly discussing what it means to us, and what style of life we should live today, in light of that reality.

IMF: What were the characteristics of that style of life you began to identify?

JGN: The main emphasis was on the word solidarity, the *hombre solidario*. People were saying how we were involved in the consumer society; and how inside ourselves, we have an individualistic and capitalist mind and aims. We have to fight this. And so the need to increase our common participation in solidarity, even in goods, even in money, in different types of possessions, became clearer. If the community is to be effective we have to change our lives, and the community should help us to change our lives.

IMF: You mean swim against the stream, not accept the popular values?

JGN: Yes; and secondly, since most of them must have engaged in political trade unions, people's associations, in the district, in the suburb, in the factory, in the area — how can we be agents of unity or encourage unity; because one of the things which preoccupies us very much is the divisions among the working-class.

IMF: Is there anything more to tell us about the groups in this area and what they said?

JGN: We shaped out a plan to be debated next year through a questionnaire. Next year we shall be discussing what it means to us to be believers in Christ and the gospel; and at the same time how this new faith should involve us in our political, temporal, trade union etc. engagement.

IMF: You've already said it was the whole people really that conducted the Mass, but I wasn't quite clear about the words of consecration. I'm asking this because in certain communities in Holland, the Ymond Community, for instance, they deliberately do not make it clear whether there is a consecration, so that those who are not christians and those who are enquirers but who want to share in the community (which, very significantly, they see being expressed most adequately by breaking bread and sharing wine, referring to the broken life of Jesus) want to partake as well. And so there is a deliberate kind of restraint at a certain point, not only not saying what's going to happen to the bread and wine but opening it out to God to do what he wants with it. Now, I wasn't very clear — I thought that you were following maybe a traditional form of service, but I wasn't clear about the words of consecration.

JGN: Usually we do that in many different ways, according to circumstances. Sometimes, as you mention, people who are enquirers come to our gathering and we don't use the prayer of consecration — but we remember what happened in the Last Supper and so on, and we say "And here is the bread, everyone will participate." Today everyone who was there was completely committed and actually the man who read the formula is a priest. He is married to a girl of our community and he is now living in the community. He prefers to use the usual formula, but sometimes we don't use it. But what we always say is that

86

when we come to the point of the words of Christ himself, it is never the priest who says that, it is always the whole community.

IMF: I was interested that the whole community said quite a bit of the liturgy together. I was also interested that probably about half the group that were there must have done a reading or made a contribution personally. That made it visible that the whole group was involved. It was an action of the group, the Mass.

JGN: Yes. And there are also different types of reading. We don't read only the Bible.

IMF: The reading was from the Archbishop of El Salvador, who was murdered: some of his reflections. And although there wasn't anything read out of the newspaper, there was reference to the news during the service.

JGN: Yes, reference to the bombing here in Spain, and reference to the economic crisis and unemployed people. Actually there are some members of the community who have been dismissed from their factories now because of lack of work. There were references to these people, as also to a member of the community who is now in hospital waiting for a heart operation. We are anxious to bring into worship day to day problems.

IMF: The newspaper, a book of testimony of Christian faith from another continent and the eucharistic readings and prayers were all together with the community's own doing and suffering in the worship.

JGN: Yes.

IMF: And that was intentional and is usual?

JGN: Yes. For instance, sometimes if there is news coming from other factories or other districts of Barcelona or Spain, or some struggle or strikes and they are put into the news, we read them out and we comment on them, because we think they belong to the common life out of the eucharist of mankind.

IMF: I was asked to bring news of other communities, and I chose to speak about the characteristics of what seems to me to be new forms of the church. Then other people commented at different times. The reflection on scripture, the sermon kind of thing, is at different points of the service and by people who just spontaneously contribute what they have seen in a fresh way. Is that right?

JGN: Yes, it is as you say, I have nothing to add to that. But after or before the consecration or the participation in bread and wine we usually invite people, or people invite themselves, to make comments on the Bible in a very spontaneous way; or they make a special prayer, or a special intention, or a special remembrance of things which are affecting them. Or if people don't want to speak they keep silent.

IMF: Now these basic groups in Spain. Are they now a

fundamental form of the life of the church? Are they widespread? Are there a great many of them?

JGN: Well, I would say there are many of them in some parts of Spain. Here in Catalonia they are in the working-class districts around Barcelona — perhaps there would be 100 communities there. Then you have a co-ordination around Madrid and in Andalusia and in the north, in the Basque country, and in Saragossa. These are the main points. We usually gather once a year, people representing different communities. For example last year, that was last December, we gathered nearly 1000 people from different grassroots communities in Spain.

IMF: And do you see any special characteristics? I mentioned ones that I personally thought were important. For instance, the search for an alternative to the church of power, the church that is allied with the power of the state, the power of the government, that feels that it has to have a recognised place and status, that has a lot of investments, that has land and has buildings, and so on. That was just the first of the points that I developed, but do you see any special characteristics that were different from the ones I mentioned?

JGN: No, I would say that these characteristics are very common in our communities. I think you have one of the documents we gave you and the last of these productions of these grassroots communities was on "What means a grassroots community in reference to the programmes of the church, a church of power, a church helping or legitimising the status quo situation politically and economically?" One of the objectives is to build a people's church. That would be one of the main things. That is why grassroots communities have grown around lower class, working-class districts, and rural areas. You won't find many grassroots communities among the middle or high classes. In the middle classes and universities, students and so on, perhaps there are some of these communities, but not so much as in the working-class areas.

IMF: In our country there was the habit that some working-class people got interested in and concerned with the church, but once they became members of the church they really abandoned their class — the church had a middle-class ambience, and they assimilated to that. Now, is it not a fresh characteristic (maybe fresh in the church in the whole of history) that what we're getting in Spain, for instance, is people who are developing the whole shape of christian life, action, worship, service, but retaining their working-class culture. Is this not a fairly new thing?

JGN: Well, there are different traditions in different countries. Here we have a type of country with a real christian tradition. . .

IMF: Was there a working-class church?

JGN: Yes, in that sense, I would say. For instance, in Catalonia, the working-class people are people who have come from the rural areas which have very deep christian traditions in a kind of folk-loric way. What has happened now when they come here and they find themselves in an industrial culture, in the struggles, strikes, and so on, is they gravitate to grassroots communities. We don't deny our origins from the working-class and we want a church belonging to the working-class. Some of them leave the church or they don't go to church because the faith they had in the country was held in a very superficial way. The people who keep their faith here, inside this new industrial culture, will never think of building a church apart from the interests of the working-class. So when you were asking if there was a church of the working-class before, I would say yes and no. The proletariat in this country grew up outside the church here in Catalonia. But the proletariat now in Barcelona, in Madrid, in other parts, has come not from the old industrial working-class who are now middle-class, but from the rural areas; and at this moment I would say there is a qualitative difference between what happened 30, 40, 50 years ago and what is happening now. Now the working-class can find a type of church through grassroots communities which links their own interests to the new reading of the gospel.

IMF: This new reading of the gospel — you talked about it earlier, and you talked about it as 'materialistic' and this is the word that is usually used. Do you mean reading it against its political and social background so that there is some impact on the political and social situation today?

JGN: Yes, that would be the explanation. When we speak of a new reading of the gospel we ask 'How do you understand' for instance 'the 25th chapter of St. Matthew?' You can read that through a bourgeois ideology and you can read that through a strike experience, a struggle experience. To read that gospel from a very engaged political way of life is completely different. That's what we mean, what we understand by a new reading of the gospel — to hear again a gospel which has been kidnapped (that would be the word) for many years by the capitalist ideology, the bourgeois ideology. We have to recover what belonged centuries ago to the people which since then, since Constantine I would say, has been kidnapped by the powers-that-be. We have to recover it.

IMF: I got the impression of being received almost like an apostle in the early church, someone who goes and sees how a local church is establishing itself and gaining strength and what its style of life is; who comes also with news of other churches so that there can be some kind of sharing. I've never had as strong an impression as that before. Was I being unrealistic?

JGN: Not at all. This was how we looked on you. I heard one comment today from one of the members of the community that it's very impressive to him to have people from such a part of the earth as Scotland coming to this little community belonging to the same faith, and bringing to us news from different small churches around the world. It is heart-warming that you were going now to visit people who are very dear to us in Central America, for whom we have a great admiration. I think that it would be a good idea if people could go around the world, since for us here it is very difficult to get this co-ordination.

Interview with
ALICE AMREIN, BIEL/BIENNE,
Switzerland, October 1984

IMF: You worked in Colombia for four years before returning to Switzerland. What kind of work did you do?

AA : The work was pastoral in character, and was with students and also with peasants in the countryside. Jose, my husband, was specially concerned with a movement of young workers.

IMF: Why return after only four years?

AA : There were several reasons, but the main one was that we belong to Switzerland and it is important that a country such as ours becomes conscientized and far more aware of the situation in the Third World. We have enough experience to be able to do something in our own country about that.

IMF: Are there links with the other groups in Switzerland?

AA : Until three years ago, there were no links. But then we started to hold an annual reunion. To start with, five or six groups took part; but last year there were fifteen groups and over an hundred prople.

IMF: And what would you call the main features of the group?

AA : Our meeting with one another is very important. We have meals together as families, from time to time in one another's houses. We have the reading of the Bible, and prayer. We have involvement in the life of the people in this area.

Every Friday we have a gathering of all the members of the group.

IMF: Do you always meet as one large group?

AA : There are two groups. We are all together every third week and the other two times the groups are separate, on the Friday.

IMF: How many people would you say were in the whole community and how many in the sub-groups?

AA : With the children we are now around twenty. But it is not so much a matter of numbers as such as the need to go deeper into things than is possible when the group meets all together. That is the reason for the sub-groups.

IMF: Does your political commitment extend only to the area in which you live?

AA : No. Recently there was a rally for peace, and each hour different groups took responsibility for leading it. Our group had an hour in that rally, which was at Berne.

IMF: Do you have an economic discipline?

AA : No. We do not have an economic discipline if that means that we share our wages, or something of that kind. But we do have a common chest, and if someone is needing time to study, for instance, we will provide a share of our income to help in that situation. It also is possible to support certain people in the Third World who need sustaining, for instance a bishop who is helping the Guatemalan refugees in Mexico.

IMF: Do you keep lively contacts with the Third World people whom you began to meet in Latin America?

AA : Yes, when people are passing through Switzerland, we get hold of them and provide an opportunity for them to meet with other Swiss, so that they can share their stories and enlarge the understanding of the people in this country. When a bishop from south Mexico visited, we were able to bring together about sixty people from this area and around. That is a fairly unusual situation in Switzerland, where people don't usually take so much interest in things outside their country.

IMF: If you were to suggest issues which European b.c.cs. should be facing, what would they be?

AA : The need for a vivid relationship with the Third World, that is one thing. Secondly, there is a need to take the measure of the role of capitalism in the world today.

But the main thing may be to begin to discover the kind of liberation which we need in Europe. I have the impression that people in the country suffer a kind of psychological marginalising. They have not come level with their own suffering, and that, I think, is why they cannot take account of the suffering of people in the Third World. It is important to pinpoint the kinds of poverty which can characterise countries which are rich, such as ours is.

We have just come to the point where we are looking afresh at the kind of commitment we should have as a group. We have our particular and personal commitments, but now we feel that the group itself should examine the kind of involvement which, as a group, should be pursued.

IMF: What about contacts with church parishes in Switzerland?

AA : One can see, on the whole, that the basic communities seek these contacts and would like to strengthen them. But in different parts of Switzerland the possibility for this varies. There are many people who have problems with the structures of the church and sometimes they find it difficult to sustain contacts with a parish at the same time as developing a different form of life in the communities.

Our group itself illustrates one kind of difficulty which is experienced because we are Roman Catholics and Protestants. We are therefore not associated with one parish but with two parishes which have different structures and different forms of life. The Roman Catholic priest shares in the group and is a good friend. The Reformed pastor knows about the group, but has simply shared once in one of its activities.

IMF: When you have a eucharist, who presides?

AA : From time to time, it is the Roman Catholic priest. But when he presides it is not in his own name but on behalf of the whole community which really is the president at the eucharist. At other times, we have people who are theologically trained but are not ordained. And a man or a woman may preside. But this is something we are thinking through carefully at this point of our own history. We are not quite sure where we are going to go at the moment. The point is that each person there has to find a way, and that will come from different positions and different histories. So we must keep thinking about how we can move forward together, as a real community. For me, personally, there is no difficulty that a woman should preside. But people with other traditions will have to think the thing through, and we must listen to all of them. The tradition and the way the church is organised makes some of these things difficult.

IMF: How do you think this will affect the church in the future?

AA : I think that ecumenism develops properly from the grass roots upwards, and the structures will change when we lay a foundation at the base, from which a different kind of practice in the church can develop.

Interview with
JIM WALLIS, 1986

IMF: Jim, you've been at the centre of the Sojourners community since it started. Have you any fresh perspectives on its development?

JW : Maybe we should think not just of our experience but of the whole movement which provides the context for our experience. When we began 15 years ago, the formation of community among us was something — as was the case around the world — that just arose within our own range of experience. We didn't know this was happening in Latin America. We didn't know anything about the base community movement in so many parts of the world. We'd never heard that language. We didn't even know what we were doing at first, we didn't call it a community! We didn't set out to build a community; we just had an experience which was a deeply bonding one which might point to the creation of a new kind of church in this country. What really happened was a conversion to the gospel at a much deeper level. Some of us were from the Student Movement, the entire world movement; some from traditional churches, some from evangelical churches, some from the Catholic church. For all of us there was a great passionate hunger for a deeper experience of the gospel and a more radical following of Jesus. That led to new community patterns all over the country — there was this emergence of a community movement, some within denominational settings and some outside, all very ecumenical even within the denominational setting. I think that community movement is facing a difficult time, partly because in reaction to the almost complete lack of community in the established church we created very strong forms of corporate life, very corporate I would say; and as we've grown older and begun families we're trying to find new forms that are life-giving and are more flexible and more sensitive to people's actual needs. I think that process is going well here. I think we have gradually been evolving towards new forms. That hasn't been the case all round the country. Sometimes when people have made the change from the very corporate communal forms — instead of finding new forms for community, they have reverted back to the old cultural forms from which they came.

This leads me to my second point, which is — I think there is tremendous pressure, cultural, economic, political pressure, that people who choose this life come under in the U.S. We are such a minority; and to live by the gospel in this culture inevitably marginalises you culturally, politically and economically. And you don't feel like you're part of a movement that is reshaping your country and your world and your history — like, I imagine, if you're in Brazil and you're in one of 100,000 basic communities and you are poor and the majority are poor and you feel like you are participating in something that really is a new reformation in the church and a whole new social revolution in that society. There, while you may be poor, while you may be suffering, you have a sense of being part of something that is very historically significant and is changing the face of your society and your world and your history. That is not something that we feel in North America. Mostly people feel small and ineffectual and marginalised and that's truly what we are. There is a movement in the churches, it's very strong, and it has been an obstacle, a point of resistance to the government, and we're in the middle of all of that: and yet we haven't won any political battle whatsoever. We have maybe been a thorn in their side. We have been a community of resistance. We've been a problem for them for we're under a lot of surveillance. We've been in and out of jail, a lot of our people have been in jail, all the time now all over the country. But you don't have the feeling that you're on the edge, on the brink of any sweeping changes either in the church or in society. That really must push you back to basic things like faithfulness being more important than effectiveness. That's true but I think for many people it's hard to live that way, to maintain that, particularly over the long haul. People can do that for a few years, five years, maybe ten years. But to live their lives this way requires a depth of faith, it requires a broader global analysis where you can feel yourself to be part of something around the world, so that you feel linked to what's happening in the Philippines and in South Africa and in Brazil. In Sojourners' case we have such deep personal friendships and relationships with people around the world, that's a lot of what sustains me. It's those connections where I feel that our part right now is to be a movement, really a movement, in resistance to the power system of the United States, which is indeed the enemy of those movements around the world. It's the power system projected out from Washington where I live that is the chief obstacle to justice in South Africa and Latin America, in the Philippines — wherever. So I think for every-day living here to always be living marginally on the edges and being more and more persecuted by the authorities, maintains itself through a system of rewards and punishments — it maintains its power through rewards and punishments — and the reward system is enough to keep most people in line. The affluence, the material rewards, their being part of cultural mainstream, their participating in the life the television says is mainstream — that keeps most people culturally and politically loyal or at least acquiescent. But when that doesn't work, when the rewards don't work, they quickly move into punishment and threat and intimidation and economic reprisal, cultural alienation, isolation or political persecution against you, going to jail and all the rest. We've organised large actions where lots of christians have gone to jail, and part of the reason is I think it's

95

a very converting thing for North American christians to go to jail. They find themselves on the other side of the law and are in jail with all the poor black people in this neighbourhood who spend so much time in jail. But I think it's going to take from us as a movement a much deeper level of commitment to maintain our lives to survive through the marginalisation and move from being a community of resistance to a place where we are actually generating the alternatives and the values and visions which will provide this country with the only real hope that it's going to have. In the end, we have to demonstrate a new and better way to live in this country, a way that can ask fundamental questions of the larger culture and can provide at least an open vision of another way to live. But I think that won't happen unless we are always, always finding a deeper faith and a deeper experience of the gospel because I think that in some ways (this is a controversial statement and people are going to be upset about it but . . .) There's persecution of the churches in the Soviet Union, in the Eastern bloc. There is terrible repression of christians and other people's consciences all over the world, all over the Third World, Latin America, Asia, Africa and so on, South Africa. But in some ways it may be hardest to live really as a christian in the United States than in any other country in the world. I'm not speaking here always of the kind of overt, visible persecution and repression that's easier to see, because I think persecution in that way sometimes strengthens and purges belief and builds up the body of Christ. You look at how vital the churches are in the Eastern bloc or in South Africa or in Central America. The greater enemy to faith than persecution is seduction, and seduction culturally, economically and politically is the great threat to the gospel. In New York, I was just told a story about Emilio Castro. He was preaching, I think, in North America and he said something like this: the North Americans and I suppose West Europeans have had just enough of the gospel to be made immune to it. There's a real point to that. We have enough of the language and the trappings and the feelings about the gospel to make us immune to the real gospel, the radical gospel, the one that we call for, that does call for fundamental changes in the way North Americans live. For those who have entered into that gospel, the real gospel, and are making fundamental changes, the loneliness and alienation and marginalisation in this culture that that brings, I think is our most serious battle. I think we would sometimes do better with real persecution than with the seduction that is a fundamental part of the way America maintains its power system. It seduces all who come within its reach, including the President of the United States. The chance before us, I think, is to see that reality more and more keenly, to see where the battle lines are, where the gospel really is at stake and then move to that deeper place and accept a marginal status. Somebody, who visited us recently, a law professor and his wife, came and worked with us for a month last summer, and they just wrote me a long letter. They talked about what it means to live on the margins for a month. That was a converting experience for them. He wrote this letter and his last line was: 'I realise now that the margin is the centre.' Spiritually, understanding at deeper and deeper levels.

IMF: I wonder if that wasn't what Janet was saying last night. She came out of a situation where there was no christian practice. Her mother was a christian of some kind but they didn't have any practice in the christian faith. I asked what attracted her to the community. She said vulnerability and fragility. She recognised people who were vulnerable and a community which was fragile and that spoke to her as none of the strong things had done. None of the hierarchical and bureaucratic and top-down things had made any impact on her to offer a way of life that made sense.

JW : The mainstream in this country is culturally, economically, politically and most important spiritually dead and bankrupt. That way of life is death. It's theologically and spiritually a dead way to live. The only hope, not just for basic communities but for this country, for this culture, is the kind of visions and values and alternatives that are on the margins. So for those of us living on the margins our task is to not be so demoralised by being on the margins but rather find the vitality while living on the margins to offer something genuinely hopeful to the rest of society.

Interview with
JANET BROWN of Sojourners, 1986

IMF: You have been a member of the Sojourners for only two months, right?

JB : Right.

IMF: You therefore have some fresh kind of picture to give. I'd like to ask you first of all, what's your own background?

JB : I'm an Afro-American. I'm pretty well educated. I'm in graduate school right now.

IMF: Do you come from a christian background?

JB : I would say yes and no. My mother is Baptist but my father was not 'observant' and so we didn't 'observe' growing up, although we celebrated the christian holidays.

IMF: So you weren't a churchgoer.

JB : No, not regularly, not until I was at college did I start regularly going to church.

IMF: What attracted you to Sojourners?

JB : A mail out to people took place and somehow my name got on the list. It took me a few months to figure out they were in Washington D.C. But I started coming to worship and working in the children's ministry. I just really liked the vision of the people, their christianity which meant seeking justice.

IMF: In 1 Corinthians 14 it says that the gauge about whether worship is real is whether an outsider comes in and finds it real. That must have been a bit like your experience; was it? You were not in on a christian community until then, and yet you came in and found the worship real.

JB : Yes I did. I found it very real. I think that the fact people were very open and tried to be very simple in their lifestyles and in their focus in worship made it real to me. I think the fact that it was rooted in a sense of our vulnerability as people and our fragility made it very real. Those are two things I remember early on in worship. I haven't got in a lot of worship experience. A lot of times you go to worship it's very hierarchical, you have the sense that that person up there behind the pulpit desk knows something no one else knows. Here I get the sense that the person is trying to discern, is just like me trying to discern meaning. They have much more seminary behind them and have had a lot more time for getting knowledge, especially in the context of community; but there is a sort of equality in all of that here, and a sense of belonging.

IMF: Can you say what impression you had of Sojourners before you came and how that relates to the impression of Sojourners once you're here? You got some kind of idea from the magazine first of all. What's the difference? Is there something deeper, different?

JB : I would say that the first thing I thought . . . . . and I didn't really have too much preconception about Sojourners when I came . . . . . the first thing I was struck with personally was that it was mainly whites, because I never knew that white people believed in biblical, justice-like theology. You see I went to a very conservative predominantly white school at the University of Virginia and a lot of the christian fellowships there were very conservative, very rooted in Americanism, I felt this was sometimes more so in christianity than outside it. To me to see that reversed by a white group really blew my own prejudice, my own stereotype of people. People were more faithful than I was used to seeing, people with a justice outlook. People seemed really more rooted in their faith and less rooted in ideology.

IMF: So the experience of the community didn't disappoint you?

JB : No it didn't and it hasn't yet. There are hard things about it — for instance working through all your economic questions, the scheduled-ness of things; but underlying all that there's just a lot of commitment to discern things together, to be whole individually and try to bring a lot of wholeness to relationships, and to love your neighbour as yourself, that's really important.

IMF: Did you find the community, fall in love with it and join it right away, that kind of thing?

JB : I worshipped with the community for two years before I joined.

IMF: So your conviction from the time you found even white people's worship real, to the point where you wanted to become part of the whole thing, that lasted two years. It was during the worship that you were sussing out the whole thing and making your discoveries, was it?

JB : It wasn't just the worship. A lot of it was working in the neighbourhood with the children's programme and realising that this was a group of people, white people, who had made a commitment to stand with a group of black people who were predominantly poor; and understanding their call to faith and their response I felt removed a lot of barriers. Having been in this country as someone with a particular racial and cultural history, a lot of what came home to me was just feeling the rootedness of the worship life, and what was going on in this neighbourhood, and feeling close to the kids especially in the programme. These feelings grew when I was commuting to and back from the suburbs to be with them on Fridays for Bible sharing. This feeling, like I had no concept of just day-to-day life with them and day-to-day life with the community and how things were coming on each day. It was both things — both the worship which gave me a real sense of a spiritual home because I'd always looked for a view of God that embraced God as loving and just, and that's very hard to find in this country. It was the worship part that grounded me spiritually. The coming into community was more just a dynamic certainty that the community was in the place where I should be.

IMF: Does the community become a real part of the neighbourhood?

JB : Yes, exactly. The community lives in relating to its neighbours. You're just wanting to be with people just as people, and having some common goals relating to what happens here in the neighbourhood.

IMF: So what was convincing was both the worship and the manner of life?

JB : Yes. Both the worship and the manner of life of the community.

THE CRUMLIN EXPERIENCE
Interview by Fr. Jim O'Halloran, 1989

The first experience I take from a big city parish in Dublin, Ireland. The area is composed largely of ordinary working people and in the current economic climate has more than its share of unemployment. The first member I interview is Ger Bailey (GB) and, then, his account is complemented by that of Dolores Connell (DC).

JOH: Ger, how did your group start?

GB : In 1982 there was a summer project for young people in the Crumlin parish. Some of those involved in that successful project built up a camaraderie and felt they'd like to go on meeting as a group. They asked advice from a young Salesian seminarist who also worked on that venture. As you'll remember, he put them in contact with yourself and you spoke of the possibility of starting a small christian community. Then, I understand, you helped them over a few months to get it started. And so a group commenced meeting at the Salesian House in Crumlin. It was composed of some of those who had worked on the summer project and others who had helped on a Salesian work camp in Co. Limerick.

JOH: Where did the experience go from there?

GB : Well, they met weekly and discussed topics such as 'community', 'justice', 'adolescence' . . . To tell the truth, they weren't too well up on these topics, but were assessed by yourself and some Salesian seminarists from the Maynooth Community. I believe you involved them, because you had to go and work in Africa and didn't want to leave the 'fledgling' community without assessment. Besides the members were all on the youthful side.

JOH: Yes, that's how it was and —

GB : There's the important point to make that in those early months those present had a sense that there was 'something special' about their experience, that something important was happening. Anyway, the community gradually grew as some friends of existing members joined. It was at that stage that I myself joined. My wife, Gemma, who was then my girlfriend, was already a member.

JOH: What about the organisation of the community?

GB : During the first year we depended a lot on the Salesians as resource persons for our community. But fairly soon they started involving us in conducting parts of the meeting — discussions, bible-sharing, or whatever. They gave us a chance to use our talents and get to know each other. I suppose they were giving the opportunity for leaders to emerge. Eventually we felt the need to choose coordinators — that's what we called them — and these were to come together and plan the meetings and activities of the group. We chose three. We felt that the coordinators could easily pick up the vibrations within the group and, by sharing and reflecting on them, help us on our collective journey.

JOH: For how long do the coordinators serve?

GB : Some change takes place in the coordinating team annually, but we never change them all at the same time. So we have the advantage of new blood on the one hand, and continuity on the other. Also with time all use their talents in the service of the community.

JOH: And decision-making?

GB : We enter into dialogue, give and take, and come to a consensus.

JOH: What sort of action, if any, did your community undertake?

GB : We were very conscious of the words of James about faith without works being dead and, consequently, about the need to **do** something. That was in the early stages. However, we were really beginning to know and trust one another. We began to think about the kingdom and what it meant to us. We thought that, rather than take up a specific work as a community, we would try to share the sense of church which we experienced in the small community with our families and friends. Our small community became a place of support, where we could share the experiences of our efforts to become more christian.

JOH: You shared your problems in the meetings?

GB : Many of the meetings were based on all we go through in our lives; our worries, sadnesses, joys and achievements. Prayer too was becoming more important to us and we tried to look at our lives and bring Jesus and the Scriptures to bear on them more.

JOH: So you complemented prayer with action.

GB : Yes. At the time, our members were becoming more involved in the wider parish community: Scouts, folk groups, CAD (Community Against Drugs), Community Enterprise (to tackle unemployment), youth clubs etc. We also tried to help another group of people start a community. This, however, did not prosper due to a fall off of interest on the part of that particular group; not a fall off of interest on our part, you understand. Again, there were some young people who had organised a summer project and wished to continue meeting (a repeat of our own experience), but sadly, the interest here also waned. We did help some folk to set up a small christian community in Maynooth College, and this group still meets. The parish curates were contacted and invited to our meetings and we organised a successful youth Mass in the parish church. On more than one occasion members of the community have gone to address school audiences about our experience. Through reflection and prayer about our successes and our failures, we felt that we were constantly learning.

JOH: Ger, would you like to tell us a little about the failures, the problems?

GB : In the time we have been together, it has happened that people have joined the community and realised afterwards that it was not for them. Early on this did not affect us too much. With the passing of time, however, when this happens, we often feel a great sense of loss. Down the years, some members have left the city altogether, or gone to a different part of Dublin to study. One of our members went to Africa to do development work, but for his own good reasons did not rejoin us on his return. Another person left to become a Salesian sister. We miss them. However, many former members still visit us, when they are around, and it's always wonderful to see them.

JOH: The pain of loss has been a problem, then?

GB : To lose a member is never easy. At one point a little group within the community were very unhappy, feeling they had been left behind by others. They thought the community was becoming too serious. During a very tense period we discussed this problem, but did not resolve it. Sadly, a few of the people who were unhappy left the community, feeling that they had been 'driven out'. At first this badly shook those of us who were left behind. But, on reflection, we felt that our community was not what was needed by those who left. This experience, as with all our ups and downs (the lot of all groups), has been part of our formation. For us the proof that the kingdom is thriving is the fact that, although smaller in number, the community is as enthusiastic as ever.

JOH: Despite some disappointment you are still optimistic?

GB : Very optimistic. The eucharist has been a great support for us. It has been an important part of our community life and a great deal of preparation has gone into our monthly celebrations. If you have faith, you can't but be optimistic can you? Some of us are also involved in the parish folk group, so we get to attend the same eucharist on Sundays. There are many aspects to our community life apart from the weekly community meetings. We frequently go out together as a group socially and have even been on holidays together. Indeed, we once got marooned on a sandbank in the Shannon for a whole night. My faulty navigating was responsible, but I was amazed at how gently the group treated me, despite the gaffe. They would have been justified in making me walk the plank. Retreats and the visiting of other groups also make up a large part of our lives.

JOH: You talk about the importance of the eucharist for your group, but what about the Word of God?

GB : It's odd you ask that, Jim. We have begun to feel that we don't bring the Scriptures into our lives enough. We think that we should now spend more time working with the Scriptures and trying to relate them to our lives.

JOH: Anything else you'd like to add regarding your experience?

GB : About two years ago, I and another member, also called Ger, went to a week-long workshop on small christian communities given by Fr. Jose Marins, a Brazilian priest, who has worked a lot with the communities. This experience proved most helpful. One of our communities is still studying sociology and another theology. Another of our people is presently on a coordinating team for a youth resource centre. The centre is used for retreats and community prayer-camps. Very recently Gemma and I brought together another group in our home. This is very important for both of us and we feel that it is a new stage in the development of the small christian communities. We have also been in contact with other communities in Dublin and beyond. Not long ago we talked with a Scotsman, Ian Fraser, who with his late wife, Margaret, has done much good work in helping to build up a network of small christian communities. And building a network is of the utmost importance for creating a sense of communion of communities. We are now in touch with a centre in Scotland that, with others, is preparing for a European Congress of Small Christian Communities in 1991. Much of the information on the communities is based on Third World experiences, but our needs and difficulties are different. We are, however, learning all the time by sharing with other communities. All the foregoing are, I think, interesting developments.

JOH: Indeed. And the future?

GB : As I said, through 'networking' we would hope to make the community of communities a reality. In our own parish we're lucky that the local clergy know us and are aware of what we are doing. We'd like, however, if the lines of communication were a little clearer sometimes. We hope that we can continue to help people on the road to community as a way of being truly 'church' as Jesus would have it.

* * * * *

(There follows the complementing interview with Dolores Connell)

JOH: Having heard Ger's account, Dolores, is there anything you'd like to say?

DC : Adding to what Ger has said about the beginning of our small christian community, I think it is important to remember that it was a very slow process. We weren't at all sure as to what we were about . . . I mean most of the experiences we had heard of, or read about, were from the developing world. And we were in the industrialised world. We didn't have the same problems. As we read about the injustices in the developing world, we wondered what **we** could do. We did feel that we had faith, but, as Ger said, we realised that the Scriptures say faith without works is dead, so there was this urge to **do** something. Eventually we agreed with one another, and within ourselves, that living according to christian values was what we should try to do. Maybe sharing with our families and in our places of work was just as important as going out and standing up for justice issues . . . Nowadays we again feel a strong urge for even greater outreach, not least where matters of justice are concerned, but that's taken six years. We are slowcoaches.

JOH: A chief in Zambia once quoted a proverb of his people for me which says: 'When God cooks, there is no smoke'.

DC : That's nice. It's like in the gospel when it says that, even when we are asleep, the seed of God's word is growing away silently. Maybe we people of the industrialised world are in too much of a hurry. We want things to happen yesterday. Time is God . . . To go on . . . In the latter part of his account, Ger refers to problems with prayer and Scripture in our meetings. But we had these problems early on, as I remember. The difficulty was how to use prayer and Scripture in a meeting and preserve a balance . . . between prayer, Scripture, and dialogue and decision-making regarding relevant issues. I mean, if we only had Scripture and prayer, we would be simply a prayer group and we didn't want that to happen . . . We didn't want to be just a prayer group. We wanted to be a community. We were afraid that we might have too much Scripture. We wanted a correct balance. Certainly we felt the Scriptures could help us live our everyday lives. At the same time there was a lot we wanted to discuss. Getting the balance right has taken a lot of time . . . Other things we've had to work on were leadership and consensus. Reading *Living Cells* we became convinced that coordination/animation was the best form of leadership. Leadership is not a question of someone out in front pulling others behind. Nor is it a question of someone behind pushing everyone in front. The leader is a person who walks **with** others and encourages them to go forward on their own steam. Our community has a team of three coordinators and this works very well . . . I must say it took us a long time to realise what consensus was all about. You see we were so anxious to bring everyone along in our decisions that a minority was in fact ruling. We didn't want majority rule, but, in trying to avoid it, we actually fell into minority rule; what we really had was minority rule and we thought we had consensus. Only in the last year or even six months have we come to grips with what consensus means. With consensus we have to agree even when we disagree. Am I making sense?

JOH: There's a little touch of Irish bull about that last

105

statement, Dolores, that people may find baffling.

DC : Let me try and take the bull by the horns, then! What I mean is that we try to come up with some decision and line of action that everyone can live with. If one or two are unhappy with what the community is favouring, they must say so clearly. They owe this to themselves and the community. Their intervention might even bring about a change. But if having listened carefully to them, the community still wants to go ahead with their decision, the two people concerned should realise that the Holy Spirit is moving the consensus in quite a definite direction and should not stand in the way. Incidentally, Ger and Gemma mentioned the problem of people leaving the community. That came because of minority rule.

JOH: How come?

DC : Well, the minority resisted the idea of greater outreach and withdrew, because the others felt they could be held back no longer. Of those that remained there were still a few reluctant to get involved in greater outreach, but they nevertheless supported the decision and so the idea of a working consensus became a reality. I don't know if Ger and Gemma mentioned 'process' and 'formation'. These were very important for us. We got a lot of guidance. After all, we were virtually all only in our late teens when the community started. Down the years, the priests and seminarians that were our assessors challenged us. Still we never felt that they told us what to do. When we decided to do something, it really came from ourselves. Making decisions for ourselves helped us to grow as a community in the past, when we were twenty members, and still does now that we are twelve. I would say that the assessors were most sensitive and respectful toward the workings of the Spirit in the group.

JOH: It would seem, then, that the minority didn't systematically hinder consensus through dialogue.

DC : Not at all. There were many decisions over which there were no problems.

JOH: Any hard feelings towards those who felt they had to leave?

DC : None. Their going was painful for us. There's no denying it. But we're still friends, still in touch.

JOH: From my knowledge of your community, I think you are shortchanging yourselves on the question of action. After all, from the very beginning there was hardly a constructive activity going on in the parish or area that one or other member was not involved in.

DC : It's true. The members were deeply involved in a whole bunch of activities: summer projects for children and teenagers, anti-drugs group, community enterprise group, group to fight unemployment . . . you name it. And yes, we probably did shortchange ourselves. But we were caught up in the idea that we should be out on the barricades standing up for justice. We didn't really see the things we were doing as action, because we did them even before the group started. It's as if you don't appreciate the gifts you have, because they are ordinary everyday gifts.

JOH: Getting truly into justice issues takes time. It looks as though you have the awareness to get there now.

DC : I hope so. But then the whole country seems to be awakening to justice. The bishops, the Council of Major Religious Superiors, and various political groups are speaking out more and more about the plight of the poor . . . From films and workshops that we've had, we've seen that small christian communities in Latin America and Africa are communities for sheer survival. They are tenaciously fighting for justice. Seeing their plight, I remember asking myself what we were doing or could do. And I thought that we must go for a simple lifestyle — not to expect to have a Porsche of our own or even the greatest house. Being thankful for what we've got and willing to share could be our way of being just to others. 'Live simply so that others can simply live', as the Trocaire poster put it. This idea occurred to me in a workshop and stayed with me. Obviously, we couldn't do what the Latin American communities did. They're in the developing world while we are in the industrialised world. Sometimes I felt that we should all imitate what one member of our community, Leo, did, and go as volunteers to Africa. We're still struggling with the whole business.

JOH: Changing the subject, if I may. Would you agree that it is fair comment to say that, right from the beginning, relating life to Scripture and Scripture to life did not come naturally to the community?

DC : I agree totally. The difficulty comes up regularly in discussions. We want more Scripture . . . no, it's not so much a matter of wanting more Scripture as how to acquire the skill of relating it to life. Of course, it's only recently we Catholics have started freely using the Word of God again. How to relate it to life is something we must seek help with.

JOH: Your community is now in it's seventh year. What has kept you together for so long?

DC : That's a difficult one. Faith, I would say. No matter what changed in individuals or the community, we all still had faith in Jesus and in christianity. We weren't always quite sure as to why we started, but we've really grown to believe in the whole idea of christian community, and definitely believe it is the way forward . . . Sometimes we wonder if it's because we meet our friends that we go to community. It's great to see your friends all the time — to be part of such a friendly lot. However, there's the other side too. It's been awfully tough at times and we stuck it out. We respect each other's feelings. Then there are those moments when you unmistakably feel the Spirit moving in the community. It happened only last night in a new small community that our group is starting in the home of Ger and Gemma. When experiences like this occur, they are truly wonderful, keep you going . . . make it all worthwhile.

JOH: And where does your small christian community go from here?

DC : We feel this urge to reach out. To establish more communities in our parish. There are a number of other discovery groups contacting us — want us to share our experience with them. This may be an outlet for setting up more communities. Then again as the members get older, they'll be getting married. Things will surely change for us. I hope, though, that we'll still be able to meet — maybe not so often — once a month perhaps. In this way we can bring christian family back again. Also I'd like if we started small communities with our neighbours in our own homes. But the present members of our small community coming together in the future as christian families is such an attractive idea. Maybe it's a pipedream. I don't know.

JOH: In many a place it's happened just as you envision it.

DC : Actually four families from the Taizé Prayer Group come together in our own parish to pray and talk about family life, so I don't see why it can't also happen for us. There's been a suggestion that we meet at Pentecost to discern our future. I think it's a lovely idea.

A SCOTTISH COMMUNITY
A group interview, 1987

EP : Our bank book says East Pollokshields Columban House. It was linked with the Columban House Network when that started, although the Network hasn't really taken off for us — we haven't got much involvement really with the Columban Houses. The nickname for the group is 'Bert's' because it's based round Albert Cross in Pollokshields. I think we're also called the Kenmuir Street group. That's okay for those who live in Kenmuir Street, but those who live in Albert Drive feel a bit miffed.

IMF: So you are Legion, you've got a lot of names! How long has the community been in being?

EP : 8 years actually.

IMF: How many are in the community?

EP : Approximately 16 adults now. 19 adults ! They grow by the week ! and 10 children.

IMF: How did it come into being?

EP : Four of us started off staying together. My wife and myself had been overseas for a couple of years and when we came back a couple of pals were staying together sharing their money etc. We were interested in what they were doing. So when we got a house we asked if they would come in with us as well. It's actually grown from there.

IMF: Is it all under one roof?

EP : No, it's not. I think there are eleven households now where single people live, couples, couples with children. So we are actually spread out over a series of streets round the East Pollokshields area, on the south side of Glasgow.

IMF: Within reach of one another?

EP : Yes, we're in easy reach of each other. There's approximately six households in the one street, just a block away from each other. It's basically in blocks we live.

IMF: Does that mean that you come together every day or every week or every month or every what?

EP : At the moment the hard and fast comings together are weekly for the whole group. The whole group meets every second Sunday and every second Monday alternately. But because we have quite a large number of adults we are also sub-divided into three small groups who meet more regularly, at least weekly, on top of those other meetings — for fellowship, for support, for meals.

IMF: How does this relate to worship? Does the worship take place in the small groups and in the larger group and in local churches. How does that work out?

EP : Well more or less that is the way it is. Most of the people are involved with the local churches. Some are involved with Gorbals Parish Church of Scotland, others with the local Baptist Church, Queens Park. Probably more than half the people worship regularly in those places. We do worship as a large group, that's the main emphasis within the group. For some of the small groups it is sort of up to themselves what they do, and some of them have chosen to spend some time worshipping together.

IMF: I'm going to ask all three of you — what is the core, what is it that holds the group together?

EP : I certainly could say friendship which is a very important thing. I think we are struggling to have other things added to that. We would like to feel that we were wrestling with what 'a simple lifestyle' means and also 'being part of a community' — trying to work that out would also be something that holds us all together; as well as issue-based work to do with justice and peace.

IMF: I'll come back to that. Would others agree that this is the core?

EP : I think I would say the main thing for me would be support in difficult things which I feel that the gospel demands. Then you need a stronger framework of support than is possible in a lot of traditional churches. This group for me does provide that deeper level of support.

IMF: Ken, would you agree with these observations or is there anything else you could put your finger on?

EP : I think what Sara and Dougie said are right. I think too there's largely a shared view of what the gospel calls us to. You tend to talk in terms of Kingdom theology. I think ideas have come to us from people like Jim Punton and through books like Chris Sugden's or *The Upside-down Kingdom*. There's what Jim Wallis is doing in Sojourners — that type of emphasis is one we feel very much at home with. Also another thing is that we do see the group as being a way to explore different ways of being church, called to be as christians living together, being together.

IMF: Do you have an economic discipline?

EP : Well, originally there was. There was a common purse. But with numbers growing, the whole nature of what people do or do not do for a living became very complex. We have a common fund that we all contribute to. We are aware of each other's incomes and we want to try and work towards a levelling of income throughout a variety of households. We contribute differing amounts to that common fund.

IMF: So you keep working at it though you haven't found a real solution yet. This is almost universally the situation in basic christian communities.

EP : It's an everchanging thing. It has not been static at all in the last five years. Change was necessary to cope with increase of numbers, with so many other dynamics, with children coming along and so many other factors.

IMF: Issue-involvement was mentioned earlier. What does that mean. Are there concrete things you get into?

EP : Yes. We try and be aware of what's going on locally. Some people have got involved with the Pollokshields Development Association. We also try and support each other if there's anything that we feel we should all be in on — represented at a demonstration or whatever. We try and do that as a group. We maybe make a banner as a group and try and get consensus on essentials. Sometimes we've had to thrash things out thoroughly. The miners' strike was a difficult one. There were different opinions. Some people didn't want the group to be associated with the strike. Some of these choices are not easy.

IMF: Would you say that (as happens in some other basic communities) what's common is that you thrash things out? You may go two different ways, three different ways, to express your own conviction. Then you'd come back and tell others how you were working it out again; you would submit yourselves to one another again. But occasionally you can be together on some action. If that's the case, then what brought you together, what have you been doing together concretely?

EP : The P.D.A. is one thing that we consider to be a whole group responsibility. It's local. Largely we're also all committed to the group 'Scottish Christians for Nicaragua' which is a support group for the Nicaraguan revolution, and which educates people about that. Most of us are involved with the Frontier Youth Trust camps for kids in the summer. We support the Accommodation Project. We're all involved in it, some more than others, as members of the back-up committee. It sets out to offer a small resource to young people coming out of care who are needing a place to live. The support worker there is part of our community, and we try to offer him support in a variety of ways. That's one thing to which the whole group has contributed.

IMF: Do you find the children important?

EP : I think it's good to have them around. One of the things we're conscious of is that if you're involved in this community you are in some way the church, it's a bit artificial in that it's a wee bit self-selected. Certainly children give you a bridge to your community life and keep your worship real. The great thing is that the children root you more in the local community.

IMF: In many basic communities children take part in the worship. But yours are too wee are they not?

EP : We have recently undergone a restructuring and one of the results has been that we have introduced a form of family

111

worship. That is on a late Sunday afternoon, and it involves the kids. The adults have found it quite a discipline to have to find and present things about the faith and stories from the Bible which children can really relate to. That has been a good and challenging experience.

IMF: Also in other basic christian communities political involvement is very much a 'must'. At the root of this is the belief that Christ puts pressure on the whole fabric of life, as he puts pressure on people personally — that ways of justice and truth might be taken. Do you, in your community, have that kind of vivid relationship between Bible study and involvement in society?

EP : Yes we do. On the night when we worship as adults, the teaching part of the worship is very relevant to life. Let me give you an example. Two of the women in the community are leading us in studies of the Bible which draw attention to the part that women have played — and this is not worked out on a theoretical basis but it leads us to look seriously at the way women are actually placed in our community and in society. We have also worked very concretely on what it means to be a christian in relation to possessions, for instance.

EP : Here's another instance. Just a week ago we were at a meeting of Evangelical Peacemakers — a number of us belong to that as well — and a representative from London took us through the biblical material from the Old Testament on war, peace and peace-making. It was really fascinating. It is the Bible that keeps on providing you with more surprises and most challenges in trying to follow a radical way of justice and peace ! It is the insights from the Bible which really tell in the end.

IMF: There's also very much a celebratory note in your worship, isn't there?

EP : Yes. In almost everything that we do as a community, we have a great deal of fun doing it, even when it's a serious thing and a task kind of thing. For instance, we have been involved recently in a lot of decorating and flitting for a family that we know — it just did not seem to be a chore at all. We often have parties. The only meeting in the year that I can think of that is not lightsome in this way is the annual review meeting of the committee. We have so much business to do there's no time to do anything but get through it. Even then, we have a relaxed evening to follow.

Interview with
Fr. ENZO MAZZI of ISOLOTTO, Florence, IMF, 1980

My first question was why it is important to establish communication between christian grassroots communities in different parts of the world.

His answer :

"The first reason given is evangelical; that the gospel is such that communities need to hear it together and make sure that they don't close themselves in in their own understanding of it, but are open to the gospel by opening themselves to one another.

"The second point has to do with the broad movement of history and the fact that at this point of history there is a new phenomenon, the emergence of marginalised people who were previously under great oppression, who had been made to believe that the making of history was not their job. They are now coming out from the shadows; they are discovering that the making of history is their job. What has become very important is that they continue to pay attention to the very local matters which they can deal with and which provide the locus for the expression of their faith, but that at the same time they become aware of this as a world movement and there is enough communication between them for them to understand what is happening in other parts of the movement.

"The third point is the experience of the group of Isolotto itself, which was able to realise, when in 1968 it became known internationally, that nowhere was there an attempt to bring a movement into being; that all the people were doing was recognising and helping to nourish and push along a movement that was in being and that in this movement people who were isolated from one another had developed forms of community and activities and an understanding of what the faith meant which resulted in some kind of Pentecost — when they talked to one another they all understood one another. In other words, the movement was one of people who were doing the same things in different parts of the world and when they did get into contact with one another they were aware that this was a world movement that already existed.

"The fourth point is that the christian grassroots communities could be picked off by those in power in the church. In a country like Brazil certain communities may feel relatively safe under an understanding bishop, whereas others are put under severe pressure and may be killed off. Those within the country, who do not see the danger clearly enough to stand with the people under threat with themselves, eventually came under threat if the bishop is relocated. On the international scale, unless there is a gathering of resources and strength to meet the attack on one part of the movement in one part of the world, that part is liable to be picked off and then different parts of the movement which feel safe in different parts of the world will also find that they are attacked.''

Father Enzo Mazzi, actively engaged in church and social reform since 1954, was harshly attacked by the Bishop of Florence, Cardinal Ermenegildo Florit, in an open letter to the press. Pressure and legal efforts were to follow when Father Mazzi and the community refused to retract their support for students investing a cathedral *(see page 73)* and to leave the parish premises.

The parish received national and international attention and became a centre of inspiration to other groups and parishes. Due to continual pressure and civil legal actions, the Isolotto community was eventually forced to leave the parish church in August 1969. Notwithstanding this it carried on its witness as believing church in the neighbourhood and continued to celebrate the eucharist every Sunday in the open square in front of the church. (Today, eleven years later, it is still worshipping there, and its latest initiative is to begin an all-European Christian Grassroots Bulletin).

.

APPENDIX
ORTHODOXY RENEWED

In the book written by Margaret and myself a few years ago *Wind and Fire : the Spirit reshapes the church in basic christian communities* a substantial section (44 close-written pages) examined the traditional marks of the church in relation to the life of basic christian communities. Those who have copies, or are near libraries which stock copies, can examine these in full. All that is possible in this much shorter book is simply to give a flavour of the section by printing parts of the material on two of these marks: "holy" and "apostolic".

When the words "one", "holy", "catholic", "apostolic" and "church" are looked at closely, I believe it will be seen that it is the b.c.cs. which represent a life-giving renewal in orthodox faith which traditionalist churches need to recover.

Caveats and Comparisons

As we proceed to examine marks of the church in relation to b.c.cs., it is well to hold in mind two traits which the b.c.cs. insist must not disfigure the church of the future as they have the church of the past.

Jesus said to the lawyers and Pharisees: "You shut the door of the kingdom of Heaven in men's faces; you do not enter yourselves, and when others are entering, you stop them" (Matt. 23:13). A church which will not acknowledge and affirm the persistent search for new life going on outside its boundaries on the part of people who do not conform to christian norms and rules, a church which acts as if it holds the monopoly regarding God's dispensing or withholding of recognition and favour to human beings, is on the way to damnation.

He also said (vv.8-12): "You must not be called 'Master'; for you have one master and you are all brothers . . . . . The greatest among you must be your servant. For whoever exalts himself will be humbled; and whoever humbles himself will be exalted." And, in Luke 22: 25,26: "In the world, kings lord it over their subjects; and those in authority are called their country's Benefactors. It shall not be so among you. On the contrary, the highest among you must bear himself like the youngest, the chief of you like a servant." The b.c.cs. looking at the history of the church note that, in spite of Jesus' warnings, the church has ordered itself very frequently as a "church of power". They are very determined that Jesus' "It shall not be so among you" shall be heeded as the church takes new shape in our day.

116

MARKS OF THE CHURCH
(a.) HOLY
1. Origin and Development of the Concept of the Holy

The word "holy" is probably of Caananite origin. Scholars debate whether the Semitic root has the connotation of "brightness" or "separation". But these may not be too strange to one another — Shakespeare gives the word "bright" a ring of menace-through-cutting ("put up your bright swords . . . . ." *Othello*,I.2.59).

"Holy" is used for what is withdrawn **from** ordinary usage and is dedicated exclusively **to** the service of a god. Initiates separate themselves **from** what is normal for common humanity and dedicate themselves **to** a way of life to which they are called (e.g. temple prostitutes, Nazarites). This "from" and "to" is decisive in understanding the concept of holy.

The word gets attached by association to places, rituals, vessels, garments, offices, functionaries, especially when priestly power is in the ascendant. "Holiness" lacks moral content in pagan and pagan-influenced interpretations. It is, there, so very material a concept that holy vessels which have been defiled need to be broken if they are pottery (as if uncleanness gets into the pores) but not if they are brass (which uncleanness cannot penetrate so readily). It is also a static concept: holiness inheres in places, practices, people.* It is a concept which, strange as it may seem, establishes areas of human licence. Those who do not invade the god's property or take for their own use what is the portion of the god and who observe the rituals faithfully, can feel they have satisfied the god's requirements and bought him off. Then the rest of life is theirs, to make of what they will.

The penetration of dualistic influences of this kind into the way of life of the people of the Old Testament is illustrated in Lev. 10: 9,10: "This is a rule binding on your descendants for all time, to make a distinction between sacred and profane, between clean and unclean." A mediating priesthood took oversight of rituals designed to express this understanding of how life should be regulated. It gave them a controlling position.

From the 8th century B.C. on, the Hebrew people had to reckon with the prophets' critiques of every attempt to base holiness on practices of religious rote and conformity. The prophets proclaimed one God who is over all the earth. He, the Holy One, is not to be fobbed off by outward appearances and ritual acknowledgement but demands justice and integrity of life from persons and communities. Sacred religious rites and customs come under fire. There is no automatic guarantee of God's favour stemming from the rite of circumcision (Deut.30: 6

---

* Note, in eucharistic worship, a range of interpretations varying between the view that holiness inheres in elements validly consecrated and that the total action is holy.

117

cf. Rom. 2: 25-29), keeping the sabbath (Amos 8: 4), worship and fasting (Isa. 58), confidence in the temple (Jer. 7: 3,4 and ff.) or the priesthood (Jer. 2: 8 ff.). In the end, all had to go. They lent themselves too readily to self-justifying religious practices.

2. Cleanliness — a Substitute for Holiness

God's demand that his people live a holy life keeps getting reduced at different points of history to a requirement that they keep pure and remain clean. Assonance contributes to the confusion (though to say so is not to ignore the sin which seeks security in impeccable observance of routines — a saying from the north-east of Scotland observes "Cleanliness is next to Godliness, and it's a damn sight easier"). The Greek word *hagios* resonates to the old Greek word *hagos* which refers to an object of awe; and to it the word *hages* the word for clean, resonates in turn.

Once forms of uncleanness were specified and graded according to their seriousness, once certain procedures for purification were prescribed, the priestly class had a weapon for control and exploitation in its hands.

a) In spite of the doctrine that God had given women and men equal dignity and had entrusted to them together the charge of the earth, women were made the chief victims of purification requirements. Their bodily functions condemned them to regular periods of "uncleanness". When a girl was born, the time of ritual defilement was twice as long as it was for a boy.

b) In spite of the doctrine that all human beings are made in the image of God (Gen. 1: 26,27), the handicapped were treated as being constitutionally unclean, and were debarred from the priesthood.

c) In spite of God's bias to the poor, the prescription that animals for sacrifice should be without spot or blemish ensured that priests lived on the fat of the land and the poor had to struggle to afford sacrificial offerings.

Came the prophets, and the very idea of cleansing was quite transformed. What was it that soiled people's hands? Not the dirt of ritual impurity. Something much more defiling. The blood of their fellow human beings. The demand for cleansing, in this context, became a demand for the establishment of justice. There was a complete reversal of the emphasis previously made. To be clean and pure in God's sight was now to accept whatever dirt stuck to you as you engaged with others in the struggle to establish God's way of life in face of many many forms of oppression. Isa. 1: 16 expresses the turn around: "There is blood on your hands / Wash yourselves and be clean / Cease to do evil / Learn to do right / Pursue justice and champion the oppressed."

Purity of life has to do not with bodies (total lives) which are stainless, but with bodies which are offered as a living sacrifice in union with Christ's. The alternative to blood on one's hands is resisting unto blood, that God's kingdom may come and his will be done on earth. 1) Baptism is entry into sacrificial engagement; it is an abandonment of the search for purity achieved through conformity, clean-handedness, an irreproachable reputation. As is said in Rom. 6: 3 "When we were baptised into union with Christ Jesus we were baptised into his death" — the death of the one who made himself of no reputation and gave up life for our redemption. 2) Baptism requires us to throw our lives on the scales for a new world. The world from which we are then to keep ourselves unspotted is life organised in opposition to God's Kingdom.

Since, for the Hebrews, the heart was not the seat of intuitive and emotional responses but the seat of thought and will and purpose, to be "pure in heart" is to have life directed, single-mindedly to doing God's will in the world.

One can see a shift in the use of the symbolism of water. Water for ritual purification could be used with the quite selfish aim of ensuring justification before whatever gods might need to be acknowledged. Jesus insisted that ritual purification was of no consequence — what mattered was one's life orientation (Matt. 15: 1-20, Mark 7: 1-23; 23: 25-28). He declared himself to be the Water of Life — refreshing, life-giving, sustaining. Out of the depth of the being of those who came to him will gush living streams for the sustaining of others (John 7: 37-39). Self-concerned longing for purity is turned around, transformed into the spending of life to refresh and sustain humanity (note the background for this in Joel 3: 18; Ezek. 47; Zech. 13: 1; 14: 8; cf. Ps. 46: 4).

Jesus' treatment of lepers and other handicapped persons and of women (e.g. the woman with the haemorrhage in Luke 8: 43-48) reaffirmed basic doctrine in face of the distortions which ideas of ritual defilement had produced.

Thus cleanness or purity, as such, is in the end given a low rating in the Bible. This is confirmed if we take into account what lies behind the Old Testament word *naçi* (cleanness as emptiness) in contrast with what lies behind the word *tam* (cleanness as wholeness and integrity of life).

"There is always an energy in the holy which is lacking in the pure and clean" (Kittel: *Theological Dictionary of the New Testament*. Eerdmans. Vol. 1, p.89). The concept of "the holy" has in it the dynamic of movement to the New Creation of God's promise. Holiness of life has to do with being in that movement, taking the risks involved.* The new heavens and earth are the home of justice (2 Pet. 3: 13); and life is entrusted to human

---

* Note, here, the contention of the Portuguese that Mary's virginity did not lie in her physical intactness but in her utter availability to God for his purposes.

beings that they may realise on earth some part of the fullness of the justice which awaits (examine here 1 Cor. 1: 9, Col. 1: 22, 1 Thess. 3: 13; 5: 23; 2 Pet. 3: 14).

Threats of the reimposition of bondage to rote and taboo had continually to be recognised and fought in the new church. Peter was converted by the enquirer Cornelius to the knowledge that, with God, nothing is common and unclean — and thus that Gentiles and Jews could be together in one church (Acts 11). Paul declared (Rom. 14: 14): "I am absolutely convinced that nothing is impure in itself . . . . .". He took the Galatians (4: 8-11) and Colossians (2: 20-23) to task for trifling with "rudimentary forces" (*stoicheia*) — which predated the change produced by their dying with Christ and rising with Him, which threatened to reimpose bondage. The writer to the Hebrews makes it clear in chapters 9 and 10 that the holy place is a place now open to all and is no longer the province of priests.

Cleanliness makes you concerned about your own state. Holiness makes you self-forgetful, committed to the fortune of God's Kingdom. In the pursuit of cleanliness, the world gets viewed as a contaminating influence. In the pursuit of holiness, the world is seen as expressing God's loving initiatives (as in the Incarnation — "God so loved the world . . . . ."). Those who take the way of holiness will be up to the elbows in conflicts and compromises, in strenuous engagement for whatever forms of justice can be realised at a particular time (this dynamic also resides in the word *dikaiosune*, righteousness) — for it is the demands and pressures of this world which provide the only appropriate milieu for growth in the holy life.

3. "You shall be Holy, for I am Holy"

The Hebrew language does not have a verb for timeless "being" only for "becoming". When God declares to Moses his identity as the rescuer of his people from slavery, the old English translation "I am that I am" proved to be inadequate to convey this purposive sense, so "I will be what I will be" stands alongside to fill out the meaning. God, regarded as a fount of being, is discovered to be a fount of purposive action. God's holiness is not expressed in some static condition of distant splendour: it is made known in liberating actions in history which reveal his saving purpose (Isa.52: 10; Ezek. 38: 16; 20: 41). Those who are called to be holy as God is holy (1 Pet. 1: 15), are to be "children of obedience", available and on their toes for whatever God shouts them in for as he seeks to bring the new order into being in the midst of the old. Those who remain determined to keep their noses clean refuse a holy calling.

The Holy One is a dynamic presence in the world. As people became aware of this, the pagan and early pagan-influenced Hebrew interpretations of God's otherness became drastically changed. God's holiness, it dawned on people of faith, does not lie in some otherness which is designed to humble and crush us, a *mysterium tremendum et fascinans* which both attracts and menaces. The otherness of God, that which makes a glaring contrast between him and other gods and between him and us, lies in what God, the all-powerful, has set himself apart **from** and **for**. He deliberately refuses the path human beings might expect a god to take. He takes a strange way for anyone to whom divinity is ascribed. The one who has all power in heaven and on earth has set himself apart **from** ways of exercising godhead which would, if we refused compliance, override our wills (and, make no mistake, God holds all the trump cards), and has set himself apart **for** a way of exercising Godhead which makes him weak and vulnerable: He will depend on human beings becoming willing partners in his purpose. The decision on God's part not to bypass us but to win us for partnership is expressed in the conclusion of the story of Noah and the flood. God will not bring human beings to heel by the threat of destruction, nor will he go back to the drawing board and produce an unfailingly obedient humanity. (Indeed destruction which we draw upon ourselves may be a sign of God's respect for us. In response to "Here am I, send me" a message may be entrusted which calls people to the Way of Life. This may meet with ears stopped and eyes closed. Then "cities waste and without inhabitant", i.e. clear evidence of the consequences of rejecting God's way, may be alone what will give human beings a fresh chance willingly to turn in a new direction, see Isa. 6).

God chooses to be "the Holy One in the midst". It goes against all human instincts that God should be seen to take such a risk. Up there he could be safe, clean, out of it, getting his way impressively. But God "in the midst", not forcing human beings to conform, makes himself incredibly exposed and vulnerable. It is shocking that the Father too makes himself "of no reputation", lays aside his glory (a word which has in it a sense of back-up from a "weight of armies"), remains invisible lest he crowd us or compel us. The way God the Father chooses to exercise Godhead is marked by the frailty of love. That is what finds expression in the visible and incarnate life of the Son.

What caused demons to see in someone who is "human as they make them" the Holy One of God (Mark 1: 24)? What caused Peter to go scrabbling on his knees among the fishing nets (Luke 5: 8) and to refuse to get his feet washed (John 13: 8)? An awareness and an awe much more profound than could be produced by the pagan sense of taboo or the Hebrew unwillingness to name the Name. The realisation that in a human being as defenceless as any other born of woman, we come in raw and direct contact with the reality of God Most High! What overwhelms us as no application of bare power can: what overwhelms us and still leaves us our personal freedom? God naked, appealing to us, bent on realising in partnership with us a new order of life.

121

If we challenge God, he can produce no evidence to convince us that one who reveals himself in such weakness is indeed God the Lord. There is nothing to back up the claim but the consistent, persistent, non-retractable investment of his power of Godhead in the salvation of the world. As Amos says (4: 2) God will swear by his holiness. It is all he has left when instruments of compulsion are laid aside. He has set himself apart **from** other ways **for** this way. The fact declares his holiness. We are called to see and believe.

4. A Royal Priesthood, a Holy Nation

Holiness is not just one characteristic among others of God's nature and of the life to which we are called. It is the energy on which life flourishes, the root from which life is renewed. When are God's people seen to meet the claim made on them "You shall be holy, for I am holy"? When they are a spring of new life in the world. The Holiness Code of Lev. 19 is quite specific. Being holy as God is holy means, for instance, leaving gleanings in fields and trees to be food for the poor, not cheating or oppressing others by holding back the day's wages of a day labourer, respecting the deaf and the blind, seeing justice done to humble and great alike.

The church is a "holy nation". That does not mean it should consist of spiritual athletes, or of people who live twelve feet off the ground; nor yet be characterised by those officially elevated to sainthood by the church (which likes to exercise proprietorial control over the values and virtues it thinks appropriate to sainthood). The "holy nation", the "people of God's own possession", comprises the ragtag and bobtail army which, with its faults patent for everyone to see, engages the enemy in his name. The saints of God, the holy ones, are a morally and spiritually motley crew. It is not merit and attainment which qualifies them. It is not unusual competence. It is simply that they are chosen and sent just as they are. It is their readiness to be chosen and sent which makes them holy people.

All these — unlikely people, many of them, to be enlisted at all — are in for a surprise when they persist in the Way. Sanctification is the gift God has up his sleeve for those who are prepared to lose life, reputation, self-fulfilment for the Kingdom's sake. They find that when they surrender life to God and offer their lives to be a living sacrifice, they blossom and flower **as themselves**. They should have known from Jesus, of course, that it is those who lose life who find it, and from John the Divine that there awaits them a new name, written on a white stone, which sums up all that they have it in themselves to be.

The kind of situation people find themselves in if they choose the way of holiness, opting to throw their lives on the scales for God's kind of world, is illustrated by the experience of an Indian pastor, contributed to the World Assembly of Christians in

Liberation Struggles, held in Spain in January 1984. He recounted how his wrestling with the biblical promise brought him to side with the people in grabbing back land which had been wrongfully seized, fighting armed police to retain it (up till then the criminal charges laid against him totalled 24); making moneylenders disgorge ill-gotten gains (one had kept a whole family in slavery for 25 years to pay off accumulations on a debt of only 100 rupees); setting up people's courts to enforce laws whose requirements were continually subverted by bribery, and women's courts which brought the powerful to trial for rape and other sexual humiliations, the women themselves carrying out the sentences.

The way of holiness is demanding and turbulent. We can bid for cleanhandedness. Or we can take the way of holiness. We must choose.

MARKS OF THE CHURCH
(b.) APOSTOLIC

The message from the Sixth Assembly of the World Council of Churches includes the following words: "We renew our commitment to mission and evangelism. By this we mean **that deep identification with others** in which we can tell the good news . . . . .". The words reveal awareness of the apostolic nature of the church's commission.

The word "apostolic" is often generally and vaguely equated with "missionary" and/or "evangelistic". But the word has its own weight.

1. In the original Greek it is used to describe seafaring expeditions, especially military. It has the connotation of "sending-in-order-to-attain-an-objective" (to engage an enemy fleet, to found a colony or such), a flavour which another word to send, *pempein*, lacks. Within this framework of meaning, the emphasis is firmly on the act of sending and being sent. Those who are sent may not even know the kind of assignment which awaits them. They are under command. They will get their orders in due course. In this way the apostle is to be distinguished from the envoy who has a clear charge to fulfil or message to convey: *angelos*, *kerux*, *presbeutes* etc. (though Herodotus used the words more indifferently).

In Cynic/Stoic thought the word is used of the divine commissioning of a human being to act as a *kataskopos*, i.e. as someone who goes where wanted and feels the pulse of ongoing life there, all eyes and ears, alert to register how human beings are managing their affairs. The work of the *episkopos* is open only to those who have fulfilled the primary function of being *kataskopoi* .

In the Greek Old Testament the word retains a great deal of its original flavour. It refers to a commissioning to go somewhere where an announcement needs to be made or a task needs to be undertaken. Some scholars (e.g. J. Y. Campbell and J. G. Davies in *A Theological Word Book of the Bible* and *A Dictionary of Christian Theology*, ed. Alan Richardson) have, I believe, too readily merged the act of sending with authorisation to represent the sender (J. Y. Campbell describes an apostle as "one authorised to speak and act for the person who sends him").

The writer of the Hebrews speaks of Jesus as our "Apostle and High Priest". Jesus was, during almost the whole of his lifetime, a *kataskopos* located in the thick of life, drinking in all that was going on around him, learning people's manifold earthy languages, sharing their daily life with its ups and downs, sharpening his judgement on a basis of deep knowledge of "what was in humanity" (John 2: 24,25). This qualified him to be our *episkopos* (Heb. 4: 14-16). He was uniquely Apostle and High Priest.

The apostle is one who is sent and available, who digs into situations and waits there at the ready. He or she can be kept on the sidelines as long as God chooses, thrown into battle when God judges the time ripe, given instructions as the battle proceeds.

In Gethsemane, Jesus' "nevertheless not my will but yours be done" was the word of God's Apostle, in the right place at the right time but sweating great drops of blood to know and to do the will of the Father. In the same way those who would be fruitful need to be like grains of wheat which **fall into the ground** and die, accepting that environment as a fertile sphere to be inserted into, available there for that disintegration which is the source of new life (John 12: 24).

A feature of Paul's apostleship is made clear in Acts 16: 6-10. He must be open to be told not to preach the Word and not to cross frontiers – activities which one might assume to be native to his missionary calling. The itch to justify the journeying, the obvious need for the untouched to hear the gospel: these do not provide sufficient justification for evangelism, they do not add up to a calling. Paul has to wait for orders. When he does make a move it is by invitation. A man from Macedonia says, "Come across . . . . . and help us". Lydia later presses him, "Come and stay with us".

Each assignment carried out returns the apostle to a state of waiting availability (there are parallels here with the Jewish institution of Shaliah, where the person sent by the Sanhedrin was authorised to act for it only for the duration of a particular errand).

Luke 9: 3 describes features of apostleship. Disciples go exposed and vulnerable into strange situations. Only if they take that risk will they find what God has for them. It will be impossible from safe ground to anticipate their assignments.

124

2. The Twelve fulfilled a representative function in the foundation of the New Israel and were without successors. The idea that they had successors is a theory promoted late in history, clearly designed to strengthen the status of the ordained. The significant number 12 was first retained by means of the appointment of Matthias to fill Judas' place; then the whole situation was prised open by Paul in his apostleship: before long the word "apostle" was adopted for many who were active in the young church as it reached into strange places or was sent helter-skelter by persecution across the ancient world (1 Cor. 15: 7).

The work of the apostle did not become an office in the church. People proved to be gifted for particular kinds of ministry; different roles had to be fulfilled to build up the body in unity; the roles were fluid within the whole ministry of the church, and could change from person to person and from time to time. Eph. 4: 11-13 points to the manner of the church's movement in mission. That movement includes apostleship, a readiness to go and be available, for however long and for whatever may be asked, sussing out the realities of situations. It includes prophecy, a willingness at the right time to bring realities thus perceived into sharp comparison and contrast with those which characterise God's Kingdom. Effective prophecy then opens eyes and thus opens the way for the announcement of the gospel. Evangelism leads to confirmation and consolidation through teaching and pastoral care. These form elements which belong to the church's mission, not an infallible process to be followed step-by-step in developing that mission.

3. Women are included in the apostolic calling of the whole Christian community. Indeed the women who testified to Christ risen from the dead are the commanding sign of the character which apostleship is to bear from the time of the resurrection forward. Before then, the number 12 provided a link with the 12 tribes of the Old Dispensation and formed a statement that the work of Jesus was not to discard but to transform the old. The Twelve represented Israel as bearing a promise for the whole world (cf. Gen. 11). They were primary sources, as those who "had been with Jesus". The continuity of Jesus' life with God's action in the past was thus affirmed and symbolised. The women at the cross and at the tomb formed a "sign forward", a sign that all peoples and all kinds of people are now called to share in Christ's ministry. Jesus' sending out of the Twelve had heralded a faith which would be for the whole world. That world dimension was made even more explicit when the Seventy* went out in mission (Luke 10). What the women made clear was that, from the time of the resurrection, apostleship becomes a mark of

* Seventy was believed to be the number of nations inhabiting the earth.

125

the whole church. The women were found where it mattered — by the cross and at the tomb, *kataskopoi* . In the course of fulfilling the normal duties which fell to women, the anointing of the body, they came up against a new reality. Events proved that they bore a constitutive hallmark of apostleship — the readiness for unexpected orders. So to them was entrusted the primary announcement of an astounding new fact. It was due to their faithfulness in apostleship, in going where they were sent, available there, that they became the first evangelists of the New Dispensation.

(Note: There is here no intention to labour overmuch the distinction between the apostle's calling as such and specific assignments which flow from obedience to that calling. When a company of people act as a body, the boundaries of particular remits get blurred, and the functions of the apostle, prophet and teacher can overlap to quite a considerable extent. But I believe that the word implies, above all, attentive and perceptive waiting and availability, and that that aspect must be given adequate attention).

The word "apostolic" retains the sense of physical movement, adds to that a movement of directed energy, entails movement into fresh geographical, cultural, class, racial fields. It can convey to us today a sense of leaving behind church-premises activities and being available in unfamiliar discovery-situations; of breaking away from known and familiar company to establish relationships with those who are in some kind of foreign territory; of being ready not only to be used to convert others but to be converted to new appreciations of God's large work in the world — as Peter the believer was converted at the hands of Cornelius the enquirer. The word implies that research and analysis should be treated as necessary disciplines to accompany commitment. Those who would be disciples are required to be teachable before the world as it faces them in that particular time and place in which God has entrusted to them the gift of life (John 1. 12,13). It is in an instructed way that they are to play their part in his transforming purpose, as those who know the scene.

The word "apostle" is a word of great courtesy and tenderness. It carries with it a sense of deep respect for other people, as and where they are; it honours their way of life, their insights, their native manner of expressing themselves, and seeks to understand and value these; it requires people to move from where they are to where these differences can be appreciated. It denotes a sensitiveness which characteristically waits for invitation, refusing to proceed roughshod into other places and other lives. It requires the believer to be open to further conversion — often coming from unlikely sources. It is a word which clarifies the distinction between evangelising and proselytising.

CURRENT PUBLICATIONS OF THE IONA COMMUNITY

THE WHOLE EARTH SHALL CRY GLORY (Paperback) — ISBN 0 947988 00 9
THE WHOLE EARTH SHALL CRY GLORY (Hardback) — ISBN 0 947988 04 1
Iona prayers by Rev. George F. MacLeod

THE IONA COMMUNITY WORSHIP BOOK — ISBN 0 947988 28 9
Iona Community

THE CORACLE — Rebuilding The Common Life — ISBN 0 947988 25 4
Jubilee reprint of Foundation Documents of the Iona Community

RE-INVENTING THEOLOGY — ISBN 0 947988 29 7
Ian M. Fraser

PARABLES AND PATTER — ISBN 0 947988 33 5
Erik Cramb

ROGER — An Extraordinary Peace Campaigner — ISBN 0 947988 38 6
Helen Steven

LIVING A COUNTERSIGN — From Iona To Basic Christian Communities — ISBN 0 947988 39 4
Ian M. Fraser

HEAVEN SHALL NOT WAIT (Wild Goose Songs Volume 1) — ISBN 0 947988 23 8
John Bell & Graham Maule

ENEMY OF APATHY (Wild Goose Songs Volume 2) — ISBN 0 947988 27 0
John Bell & Graham Maule

LOVE FROM BELOW (Wild Goose Songs Volume 3) — ISBN 0 947988 34 3
John Bell & Graham Maule

LOVE FROM BELOW (Cassette) — No.IC/WGP/008
Wild Goose Worship Group

CLOTH FOR THE CRADLE (Cassette) — No.IC/WGP/007
Wild Goose Worship Group

A TOUCHING PLACE (Cassette) — No.IC/WGP/004
Wild Goose Worship Group

FOLLY AND LOVE (Cassette) — No.IC/WGP/005
Iona Abbey

FREEDOM IS COMING (Cassette) — No.IC/WGP/006
FREEDOM IS COMING — ISBN 0 947988 49 1
Utryck

MANY AND GREAT (World Church Songs - Volume 1) — ISBN 0 947988 40 8
John Bell & Graham Maule

MANY AND GREAT (Cassette) — IC/WGP/009
Wild Goose Worship Group

PRAISING A MYSTERY — ISBN 0 947988 36 X
Brian Wren

BRING MANY NAMES — ISBN 0 947988 37 8
Brian Wren

WILD GOOSE PRINTS No.1 — ISBN 0 947988 06 8
John Bell & Graham Maule

WILD GOOSE PRINTS No.2 — ISBN 0 947988 10 6
John Bell & Graham Maule

WILD GOOSE PRINTS No.3 — ISBN 0 947988 24 6
John Bell & Graham Maule

WILD GOOSE PRINTS No.4 — ISBN 0 947988 35 1
John Bell & Graham Maule

WILD GOOSE PRINTS No. 5 — ISBN 0 947988 41 6
John Bell & Graham Maule

EH... JESUS... YES, PETER...? Book 1 — ISBN 0 947988 20 3
John Bell & Graham Maule

EH... JESUS... YES, PETER...? Book 2 — ISBN 0 947988 31 9
John Bell & Graham Maule

WHAT IS THE IONA COMMUNITY? — ISBN 0 947988 07 6
Iona Community

CO-OPERATION VERSUS EXPLOITATION — ISBN 0 947988 22 X
Walter Fyfe

COLUMBA — ISBN 0 947988 11 4
Mitchell Bunting

FEEL IT — Detached Youth Work In Action — ISBN 0 947988 32 7
Cilla McKenna